Reflective Playwork
For all who work with children

Jacky Kilvington and Ali Wood

continuum

Continuum International Publishing Group

The Tower Building   80 Maiden Lane,
11 York Road   Suite 704
London SE1 7NX   New York NY 10038

www.continuumbooks.com

© Jacky Kilvington and Ali Wood 2010

Every effort has been made to trace copyright holders and we apologise in advance for any unintentional omission. We would be pleased to insert the appropriate acknowledgement in any subsequent edition.

British Library Cataloguing-in-Publication Data
A catalogue record for this book is available from the British Library.

ISBN: 978-0-8264-9764-2 (paperback)
        978-1-4411-6768-2 (hardcover)

Library of Congress Cataloging-in-Publication Data
Kilvington, Jacky.
Reflective playwork: for all who work with children / Jacky
Kilvington and Ali Wood.
    p. cm.
ISBN 978-0-8264-9764-2 (pbk.) -- ISBN 978-1-4411-6768-2 (hardcover)
1. Play. 2. Play--Philosophy. 3. Child development. 4. Creative
ability in children. I. Wood, Ali. II. Title.

LB1137.K525 2010
649'.5--dc22

                                                      2009011852

Typeset by Newgen Imaging Systems Pvt Ltd, Chennai, India
Printed and bound in Great Britain by CPI Antony Rowe Ltd, Chippenham, Wiltshire

Contents

Foreword

We are two women who via various circuitous routes of work with children and young people eventually ended up in playwork – partly because we both deeply believed in the life-force that is play and also because we felt strongly about a child's right to be and to have a sense of self that makes life worth living. The playwork sector was where we found like-minded people who are also fascinated by the amazing capable and creative people children are and who care very much about the damage being done to children in the UK society in name of education and protection. We are both now well past middle age – a fact we and others close to us have trouble believing – but we still feel very much at home in playwork as a profession, despite the many challenges this continues to bring to us both.

We are writing this book together because (a) we are both far too self-critical to have ever managed to do it alone and (b) while we share the same passion for children's rights to play, we still have different experiences and perspectives that we felt were worth more together than apart. We share with you here a little of ourselves as individuals and how we got to where we are and while we will mostly use the editorial 'we' throughout the book, we will identify where we contribute our own stories.

Jacky

What brought me to this point of writing a book about reflective playwork with my friend and colleague Ali? I, like you, was once a child. Happily I had a loving family upbringing and a rich play life, mainly played out in my head and in my home and big old garden and in various other homes and gardens. I was not allowed to play in the street or walk to any local parks or free ground alone or with friends, until I was well into my teens. This did not stop me climbing and swinging in trees, jumping off garage roofs, making mud pies, making dens, playing with water, walking on stilts, playing tricks on people and so on. I lived with an extended family of parents, sister, grandparents and an aunt, uncle and cousin, in a big old Victorian house which was the perfect venue for hide and seek; murder in the dark; playing make-believe games and all forms of imaginative and creative play. I remember many Sunday afternoons, after Sunday lunch, when my sister, cousins, friends and I would assemble a sleepy crowd of relatives, charge them a penny or two and put on a variety of shows of the magic, musical, dramatic or humorous variety and perform, suffer embarrassment, argue and laugh to a snoozing audience of adults, or failing that to an imaginary audience. Reflecting back I realize that I was lucky, I had a permissional play environment where children playing was encouraged and supported. My mother used to provide us with the props for dens and my father, who was a printer, provided us with huge quantities of big paper that we could paint and draw on. We were encouraged to invite our friends home and we were allowed to hide on top of and in the big old cupboards; put music on to dance to; make a mess in our bedrooms, as long as we cleared it up; read comics and books; use paints, scissors and glue and we were left alone to play. I only played with other girls until I was in my teens. Reflecting back I realize this experience has had an effect on my views about play and the importance of play provision for children.

After leaving school and a brief stint as a secretary, I trained to be an art teacher and became a teacher, wife and later a mother of two daughters. After time, a change to youth work and further education, a change of partners, another child, a son, another husband and two step-daughters, by luck I was asked to be involved in the development of a new nationally recognized qualification in playwork. To do this I had to become involved in the practical as well as theoretical side of playwork and it fitted me like an old dressing gown. I realized I had found my niche. At last here was a profession where relationships with children were authentic, where power was not an issue. Where children's innate creativity did not have to be harnessed to specific outcomes or channelled into regulated frameworks. I was able to use my knowledge of the education requirements alongside my new and growing knowledge about play and playwork to do several things. One was to develop and co-ordinate college playschemes for the children of lecturers and students during school holidays. Another was to develop and write a number of playwork courses at different levels and for and with different organizations. Yet another was to produce teaching materials for some of these and then teach them either as part-time courses or as modules on leisure and recreation courses. I became involved in many different developments related to playwork both locally in Sheffield and nationally including the national vocational qualifications in playwork; the first playwork degree and a play policy and strategy for Sheffield. Following early retirement I became an out of school co-ordinator and a casual playworker for the local authority. I went on to work in a community childcare centre which offered playwork and childcare for local children and training for their families and other local people and it was here that I learnt about playwork within a community and about the relationships between playwork and many other professions that work with children. I now have three grandchildren and I owe a huge debt of gratitude to them and my own children for giving me the opportunity to gain a wonderful insight into their worlds and their playing. This has kept me grounded and ensured that I see children in a 'real' light and not in some 'fluffy' sort of way.

Throughout all of this personal history within the world of play I remain firmly committed to 'the playwork way' of working with children. My reflections on my own childhood; my experience of being a mother and grandmother, and of working with children, as a teacher, youth worker and playworker; my interactions with playworkers and other people who work with children; the research I have carried out related to play and playwork for the purposes of developing and writing for playwork, all convince me that in our modern environment where children's lives are so constrained or so misunderstood, playwork provision provides a haven for play and playworkers using a playwork approach support children to be who they are meant to be.

Ali

I was the middle child of five. My mother was a teacher and one of the first working mothers in my generation (how ever did she cope with a job, five children, no automatic washing machine, no supermarket and only one coal fire downstairs?) and my father managed a factory and worked hard so I was definitely shaped by the whole work ethic. I struggled somewhat to find the place of 'best fit' between two older brothers and two younger twin-sisters as I was growing up, playing with the boys in the woods and on building sites and role-playing with dolls and my sisters. I read avidly as a child and wrote reams about my thoughts and questions, which were fuelled by the death of a cousin my age and the murders of three girls on Cannock Chase. I remember spending a lot of time thinking about what life was for and trying to make sense of it all through 'what-if' games and a rather reckless approach to risk-filled play. Like all children, I felt most alive when playing and relished the feeling.

My father's sudden death when I was thirteen blew my world apart and finding answers then became a mission throughout my rather tumultuous teenage years set against the backdrop of the late sixties and early seventies. It was a heady and confusing time and resulted in my leaving home to live in a religious commune for several years until the cult it became finally imploded. It was there however that I learnt so much about the good, the bad and the ugly in other human beings and in myself and those years set the scene in my wanting to work with people.

I had not chosen wisely or done too well in my A-levels and so in an attempt to be different and reshape the expectations others had of me I went off and trained as a secretary and learnt many skills I still need and use. Throughout the years in the community I had various secretarial jobs but ended up working as a medical secretary in the Children's Hospital. My boss was a consultant haematologist and so treated children with leukaemia and other life-threatening illnesses. Once again I was thrust into close contact with the stuff of life and death and the ways we all try to live with this.

In the better times in the community we were pretty creative and wrote and performed songs and theatre pieces. Later on when we got more outward looking and involved ourselves more in our local neighbourhood, we got to know local families and young people and involved ourselves in initiating support groups and activities and even community musicals. These experiences, coupled with those supporting children and families at the Children's Hospital convinced me to go and qualify in something people-related and at the end of the community's life, I ended up at Westhill College doing a youth and community work course. This was utterly life-changing and both added to and greatly expanded all my still-not-answered questions. Over the next several years I had a ball working as a youth, community and/or playworker in a variety of settings and organizations which included running youth clubs, doing detached work, setting up a community farm and community arts projects, co-ordinating playschemes, developing credit unions and campaigning for local play space. Along the way I unexpectedly had a son (now a playworker himself) and becoming a parent with all its agonies and ecstasies prompted whole new perspectives and queries.

Already personally inspired by learning I enrolled on a degree and then a master degree course and also began to get involved in training others to become workers in the youth, community and play sector. I also got married and inherited two stepdaughters and as if being a new stepfamily wasn't enough for us, my new husband and I also became foster carers. In retrospect I think I muddled my way through most of these years in a constantly enquiring state!

Over time however, this heady mixture of working, caring, playing and learning slowly began to crystallize and focus my thinking and helped me find my 'home' which is very much in the playwork sector. I feel deeply about children's right to play – playing is fundamental to our sanity. It gives laughter, provokes curiosity, enables experimentation, gives opportunity to find friends and recognize 'enemies' and gets us thoroughly in touch with what it means to be human. I find it endlessly fascinating watching children play and trying to see the world through their eyes and how they shape it – because shape it they will.

I currently spend a lot of my time involved with designing and delivering national playwork qualifications because my other fascination is with how and why people learn and how we can consequently inspire other people to 'get' the playwork approach. This involves a lot of thinking, a lot of writing and a lot of meeting and working with some fabulous people from whom I have also learnt much and a lot of arduous meetings and often frustrating procedures in the long process of trying to get it right at different levels.

Learning and playing are both different and similar – they both inform each other. Learning about play, playwork, oneself and others (for these are all interconnected too) should be a real experience with highs and lows and eureka moments and times of quietly growing recognition of what this all means in practice. I have to say it's become a bit of a mission to try to influence the various powers that be, that getting qualified as a playworker (and as a playwork trainer/assessor/lecturer) should be a far-reaching and playful journey in itself. But although it is not without its head-banging (and even table-banging) moments, I'm gaining insights as well as friends and colleagues and having a lot of fun along the way!

As for my personal quest in finding answers, I have become content with knowing that while a few answers sometimes unexpectedly present themselves, most of them will never be known. I can live with the questions now, even though they continue to deepen and broaden.

Writing this book has been somewhat of an expedition in itself. We both work within playwork education and training and so wanted to write about what playworkers need to know, but also about what that means in practice and what impact that has on both adults and children. We have called the book 'Reflective Playwork' because true playwork cannot be done without the feelings, questions, challenge and debate that are part of reflective practice. We have tried to be honest and include here and there anecdotes from practice and examples of our own deliberations and failings. We have laughed, debated, sworn and struggled with several chapters and still feel they are unfinished but perhaps this is as it should be.

So we invite you to tread lightly but deeply through these pages and begin by posing this thought.

> Eating is about a number of things – satisfying hunger, shared experience, creativity, addiction, experimenting, physical digestion, giving, receiving – It is not necessarily all or even some of these things at any one time and long-term concentration of just one of them can take away from the whole experience.
>
> Sex is also about a number of things – procreation, physical satisfaction, expression of love/commitment, mutual experience, self-esteem, personal power, discovery, angst – It is not necessarily all or even some of these things at any one time and long-term concentration on just one of them can skew the whole thing.
>
> So too with play – play is about survival, all-round development, evolution, learning, catharsis, invention, identity, discovery, the meaning of life – It is not necessarily all or even some of these things at any one time and adults making any one of these more important than another will create imbalance that leads to deprivation.
>
> We all of us need to seek to understand, promote and keep this balance rather than compete with different rhetorics and theories. A good playworker gains and keeps gaining through reflective experience the understanding, self-awareness and ability to know when to keep away (from children playing), when to respond, when to intervene, when to 'spark', when to create, what effect s/he is having – All of these things in reality are part of the very complex and sensitive role of the reflective playworker.

Read on!

Acknowledgements

We owe thanks to numerous people for numerous reasons and if you believe we owe you thanks and you are not mentioned by name in this section please accept our invisible gratitude.

Thank you to Perry Else without whom we would not have been given the contract to write this book. A special thanks to Steve Chown who read early parts of the book and gave us incredibly helpful feedback. He is a star! Thank you to all the writers and theorists of all the works that we have dared to refer to or cite from; you have been an inspiration and we hope we have done your work justice.

Every effort has been made to try and trace copyright holders for all materials and quotations used. If we have made mistakes we apologize and the necessary arrangements will be made by the publishers if they are alerted.

Thank you to all the people who supplied us with photographs of children playing and with permission for their use in this book:

> Thanks to Nancy Alford of Contrast Photography (www.contrastphotographyuk.com) for her beautiful images (1.1, 2.3, 2.5, 4.1, 5.1, 5.3, 6.1 and 7.1) and also to the 'Apex Challenge' whose participants are featured in three of these images.
> Thanks to Sue Smith (2.1, 3.1, 4.2, 5.2, 9.1)
> Debbie Willetts and Ian Smith (8.1, 3.3)
> Tilly Mobbs (1.2, 2.2, 2.4, 3.2, 6.2, 8.2)
> and all the children who featured in their photographs – Sean, Adam, Mali, Fern, Ashley, Abigail and Lewis.

We may now sound like we are moving into Oscar-impersonation style, but can assure you this truly is heartfelt – thanks to all the children that we have ever worked with or known and particular thanks to our own grown-up children, stepchildren and grandchildren with whom we still play. At various times you have all kept us in touch with the real world of childhood.

Thanks as well to all the people with whom we have ever engaged in debate about children, play and playwork. You have kept our minds lively and the questions coming.

Particular thanks to our long-suffering partners Pete and Dave who have given us various technical and moral support. Finally we would like to thank each other for at times making the process of writing such fun and at other times supporting each other to keep going when the going seemed too tough.

Introduction

There are two things to be considered about this book before you begin to read further.

First, while it is about playwork, it is not just aimed at studying or practicing playworkers. The book contains theoretical, practical and reflective material that will be useful for anyone working with children because it talks about play, which is universal to all children and therefore something we could all better understand; and it also talks about the playwork approach, which we believe can be used by parents and carers and by other professionals in the children's workforce. The book will additionally be useful to those other professionals who want to understand more about playwork itself – what it is, why it exists and how it is managed and informed.

Second, it is very much about *reflective* playwork and by this we mean that it requires us as writers and invites you as readers, to think more deeply and critically about our work with children. In many fields of work, physically 'doing the job' often takes priority and buries the potential for improvement and discovery along the way. In these pages we want to reverse that trend and unearth learning by questioning more closely what we each do, see, think and feel in our own work.

We should additionally explain the following to help you both navigate the book itself and understand some of our terminology.

a Playwork is a fast-growing and developing field and there is much research and theorizing currently taking place. We will be referring to both emerging and more established theory and hopefully demystifying (and questioning!) it all.

b Each chapter is relatively self-contained and its title self-explanatory so, in the main, can be read alone or in a different order than that given here.

c References to relevant websites and/or books are given at the end of each chapter so that readers may follow up and/or explore certain aspects of theory or practice further.

d Our use of the terms 'child' and 'children' does refer to any and all children and young people of school age in the United Kingdom, whatever their individual background and circumstances.

e Our use of the term 'playworker' refers to both those employed or working voluntarily in the playwork sector and those adults who perhaps – knowingly or unknowingly – use a playwork approach when relating to children of any age

f 'Play' is understood and interpreted by diverse people in a myriad of ways – as Chapter 2 demonstrates. Playwork however, sees and feels play – as far as is possible for adults – through the eyes and hearts of children and that often surprises, shocks, confuses and delights us at different times. It really does take courage, honesty and openness to see their world from their perspective.

There are many times when we feel we should leap in there and do or say something, but this is usually because we have not understood the depth and breadth of children's play lives and the deep necessity they have to play out their experiences, emotions, dreams and questions in instinctive ways we have forgotten or no longer need to do.

So this book has nine chapters that cover various aspects of playwork. Each chapter will have some of our own reflections and will also pose some reflective questions to stimulate the readers' thinking.

Chapter 1 explains what playwork is and is not and outlines how the Playwork Principles underpin the role of the playworker. Reflective practice is described in detail as one of the most important processes of playwork.

Chapter 2 is all about play. It takes a look at a variety of old and new and sometimes competing, theories related to play and outlines how playwork researchers have and still are adapting and developing these in order to create a coherent framework for playwork practice.

Chapter 3 outlines the new paradigm for play that has been developed as a result of the ongoing research and describes the contents of the emerging 'coherent framework' that informs modern playwork practice.

Chapter 4 is all about the child – the 'guinea pig' of so much adult thought and attention. We have tried to give a fair and balanced historical account of how the modern child has come to be viewed in the way that she has and to consider how views about children and childhood, influence the way that adults including playworkers, work with children.

Chapter 5 looks at the main practice of a playworker (other than reflective practice) as being; to enable children to create play environments so that they can play freely; provide play materials that support a wide range of play behaviours; observe children playing to gain information about play; intervene if and when necessary to support the play process.

Chapter 6 considers how legislation and external systems impact, positively and negatively on playwork practice and the play of children and outlines some of the most important aspects of current policy.

Chapter 7 is all about quality and management. It describes the quality measures that are used to assess playwork practice and considers the positive and negative effects that the use of these can have. It also considers issues that are specific to managing playwork.

Chapter 8 describes the relationships that exist between playwork and other professions that are involved with working with children. It also considers the relationship between playworkers and parents and carers and tries to imagine a world where children's play (and therefore playwork) is fully appreciated.

Chapter 9 is about building a trained and qualified play/workforce. It looks at the importance of continuous professional development for playworkers and considers how knowledge of learning styles and playful training could help to broaden the understanding of play and playwork.

Delve in, folks!

Principled Playwork

Chapter Outline

What is playwork?

Out of all the professions where people work with or alongside children, playwork has to be the most misunderstood. The very word – joining together two other seemingly opposite words, probably doesn't help! Most people have a good idea of what a teacher or a child-minder does and why, but this cannot be said for playworkers. This however, doesn't stop people surmising or thinking they do know!

Let's put the record straight. Playwork is a relatively new profession (as is childcare) and despite its importance, one that is not recognized as such in many circles. It began with its roots in urban community work in the late sixties and early seventies on unused local land – the workers then saw themselves as having a variety of roles (parent, teacher, advocate, social worker, police officer, etc.) because they immersed themselves in local children's lives. It was however, this immersion that for many slowly prompted a greater understanding of play and its huge importance to and impact on children. This in turn created a growing recognition that play itself and the right to freely play, was to be guarded and supported if children were to survive in a changing world.

The term 'playwork' began to be used in the eighties to describe a distinct way of working with children on the unused land that then became children's playgrounds.

> Leading a playground is not like leading play and occupation. The children are sovereign and the initiative must come from them . . . to organise and arrange programmes is to stifle imagination and initiative and preclude children whose lively curiosity and interest demanded new outlets. We should

not forget that play itself is a natural process, shaped by the child's own interest at any given time and the possibilities offered by any given environment . . . no matter how we might consider play potential in our present and future design, children will continue to interpret this in their own way. (Benjamin, 1974:1&3)

Playwork continues to evolve, with an ever-increasing theoretical foundation and supported by academics in a variety of other fields. Its original passion for children's rights continues to fuel it – sometimes quietly, sometimes loudly – and to champion that which children themselves see as imperative to them – play.

Playworkers are quite a diverse group – they often debate and disagree with varying levels of passion, but this is not uncommon in a new field of work and in many ways it is very healthy. We do however, have some parameters that have been developed, consulted on, commonly agreed in the field and then endorsed by SkillsActive – the Sector Skills Council responsible for playwork training and qualifications. These are the Playwork Principles, which are listed below.

Playwork Principles

These Principles establish the professional and ethical framework for playwork and as such must be regarded as a whole.

They describe what is unique about play and playwork, and provide the playwork perspective for working with children and young people.

They are based on the recognition that children and young people's capacity for positive development will be enhanced if given access to the broadest range of environments and play opportunities.

1 All children and young people need to play. The impulse to play is innate. Play is a biological, psychological and social necessity, and is fundamental to the healthy development and well-being of individuals and communities.
2 Play is a process that is freely chosen, personally directed and intrinsically motivated. That is, children and young people determine and control the content and intent of their play, by following their own instincts, ideas and interests, in their own way for their own reasons.
3 The prime focus and essence of playwork is to support and facilitate the play process and this should inform the development of play policy, strategy, training and education.
4 For playworkers, the play process takes precedence and playworkers act as advocates for play when engaging with adult-led agendas.
5 The role of the playworker is to support all children and young people in the creation of a space in which they can play.
6 The playworker's response to children and young people playing is based on a sound up-to-date knowledge of the play process, and reflective practice.

7 Playworkers recognize their own impact on the play space and also the impact of children and young people's play on the playworker.

8 Playworkers choose an intervention style that enables children and young people to extend their play. All playworker intervention must balance risk with the developmental benefit and well-being of children.

We will enlarge on and refer back to different principles at various times, but here give an overview of what they mean.

The first two principles set the scene in that they attempt to describe what we currently accept about play. Daroon stated 'Attempts to characterise or define play are legion; a concise definition seems almost impossible' (1977:123) and thirty years later, the various theories about the origins and benefits of play are of course still being examined and the perspectives that gave rise to them (many of them socially or politically constructed) challenged. The next chapter goes into more detail on this. The 'changing fashions in the definitions of play . . . have coloured our adult conceptualisations' (Sutton-Smith, 1986).

Key question

Why do children play? Much evidence suggests that play is actually a biological drive and is therefore as fundamental and necessary to children as eating and sleeping. What do you think?

The first two principles are inevitably but also unashamedly from an adult perspective, because they have been arrived at via four routes; by adults using

a their intuition,
b their personal childhood memories,
c their experiences of working/being with children in play situations, and
d what they have gained from whatever research and other data or evidence they have read (Hughes, 1996:30).

We cannot say that these first two principles are therefore accurate, but as a whole they set the stage in defining what is important for us adults to understand about play if we are going to be around children playing. The reality is that children absolutely do not want adults to control or direct their play – adults 'get in the way, spoil everything and just don't get the point' (one articulate seven-year-old in 2006).

Reflection opportunity

Recall memories of you playing as a child. Where were you?
Who were you with? What were you doing? What were you feeling?
What were you playing with? What were you sensing?
How did the play stop on that occasion?
What does all this tell you about play?
Do your play memories 'fit' Principles 1 and 2?

Over the years we have asked thousands of adults of all ages about their memories of playing and there are many commonalities. The vast majority (apart from some young adults whose freedoms were more limited) over and over remember playing outside, playing made-up games, playing with whatever was to hand and playing away from adult eyes – all of which expound the first two principles well.

Principles 3–8 go on to describe the basic inter-related aspects of the playwork job, that is, what underpins whatever a playworker does. There is no 'right' way to do it, no blueprint or job description to conform to. The Principles describe an approach, an attitude, a belief system, a way of working that is very different to other ways of working with children. It is an approach that is instinctive and natural for some people (in other professions too) but also can be learnt through reflective practice. It is an approach any adult can understand and use in their work with children at different times – the only difference being that professional playworkers use it all the time. To use the old adage – 'it's not what you do; it's the way that you do it'.

Essentially, a playworker understands that children's play is very much their domain; adults are not wanted unless:

some predicament or disaster occurs;
some kind of assistance is required;
there are no other children to play with; or
the adults are sufficiently playful and intuitive and follow children's lead if invited.

The playworker therefore is primarily a bystander who proactively supports play through:

1 seeking out and helping create specific places where play can happen (because children are not often allowed to do so themselves)
2 ensuring these places have sufficient and varied components and props that truly interest children
3 unobtrusively observing play, thereby learning more about play and how to better support it
4 sensitively judging when and how it might be occasionally necessary to intervene (e.g. to prevent serious injury).

None of this is easy. It goes against much of what we feel as adults 'responsible' for children.

It also means that more than any other adult, playworkers get to see and know children 'in the raw' – a rare privilege not to be taken lightly or abused. Parents feel they know their children, but in reality, if they could peak through a two-way mirror and see their offspring playing with peers, they would probably not recognize them.

Playworkers can use the insights and understandings they gain to advocate for children's rights and to educate other adults about children's real needs, relationships, development and culture and particularly about the importance of play in its multiple forms for survival, identity, expression and growth.

So playworkers do *not* exist in order to:

1 correct or control children's behaviour;
2 ensure children never come to harm;
3 entertain children;
4 lead or direct children's play;
5 plan activities for children;
6 teach children what they need to learn;
7 socialize children into being good citizens;
8 look after and protect children.

Although these are normally all roles undertaken by and expected of adults responsible for children.

This does not mean playworkers are irresponsible or uncaring, or that they do not sometimes do some of the things listed above. It means there is a great shift in emphasis and that responsibility and care is expressed differently. Playwork is unique because its fundamental reason for existence is to support play. And play is what children prefer to do away from adults. Do you remember? Adults got in the way, stopped you, told you off . . . and yet you knew – with great certainty and intensity – that what you were doing was vital and important and they just didn't understand . . .

Key questions

Do you still play as an adult? In what ways? Who with? Why?
Is adult play different to children's play?
Might that colour your view of children's play?

It would be true to say that many people, both employing and even employed as 'playworkers' have still not understood this and see the role as primarily one of group child-minding and/or activity leadership. Playwork is however neither of these things – playwork serves and supports the play needs of children *as defined by them*.

Photo 1.1 Free to play.

Why are playworkers needed – if they are needed at all? Put simply, times have changed. The majority of children in this country have far less freedom and mobility than they did a few decades ago; children then played out for hours on end, only returning when too cold, wet or hungry or when called in. Most children today have little time away from adult eyes and adult control and spend much more time indoors where they are deemed to be 'safe'. There is now little doubt that this situation has taken its toll on children's development, independence and health and well-being. At no other time in these islands have children had so little freedom. They are 'increasingly battery-raised – cooped up in their homes, living virtual lives, or in the car, being transported – rather than enjoying the free-range existence they could expect even twenty-five years ago' (Palmer, 2006:62) and concern is growing in a number of related professions at the effects this is having. On the other hand there are also those children who are at risk of real harm because they are left to play out anywhere in what is now, in some urban areas, a hostile environment with more cars, more access to drugs and less community interest.

Playworkers therefore create 'compensatory play spaces' – places that give children back their freedom to play in the ways they need and want. Ideally such places comprise both outdoor spaces (open to the elements and both wild and landscaped) and a variety of indoor spaces that children genuinely feel is theirs.

Photo 1.2 Hidey-holes inside.

Sadly many play settings fall short of this and are operating where there are many constraints and many adults who do not understand children's need – and right – to play. Such adults often have good intentions but in reality they at best inhibit and at worst prevent play, by insisting on certain rules, behaviours or environmental conditions.

Play settings technically include anywhere where children play, but staffed and supervised play settings could include any of the following and be either 'open access' (i.e. children come and go as they please) or closed access (children are booked in by carers who usually bring and collect them):

1 before and after-school clubs
2 playschemes
3 mobile play projects
4 adventure playgrounds
5 playcentres
6 junior youth clubs
7 parks and streets 'staffed' by play rangers

This does not mean however, that every after-school club or playcentre for example, will be effectively playworking. Much depends on sympathetic and supportive management, the training the workers have received and their attitudes to children.

Reflection opportunity

Think about settings you know. Are children really free to play there? Can they play outside, make their own choices, get dirty, explore and experiment . . .? How do the workers behave – do they support or restrict play? What is the priority there? Is it children's safety? Parent's views? Job requirements? Or is it play?

Reflective practice

Before we move on to the next chapter, we need to say a little more here about reflective practice – what it is and why it is so important for playworkers. Many think that reflective practice just involves thinking back and evaluating 'how something went'. It is much more than that. In many ways, playwork is an 'unnatural art' with a 'whole raft of tensions and contradictions inherent in what we are expected to do' (Russell, 2005:98).

Trying to support the play needs of each individual child, whatever their personal needs and preferences, personality type, previous experiences, expectations, age, gender, ability, culture, social status, language, economic condition, race or nationality is an almost impossible task, not least because it also constantly hits all our protective and educative adult buttons where we find ourselves wanting to control, organize, sort out, teach, look after, keep safe, remonstrate when children do not want or need us to do so.

So reflective playwork is not just about thinking about what happened, weighing up what was good or not-so-good about it and consequently deciding what to do next time – as in the following diagram.

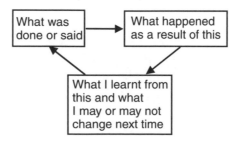

Figure 1.1(a) 'Single loop learning'.

Reflective playwork however, looks more like this:

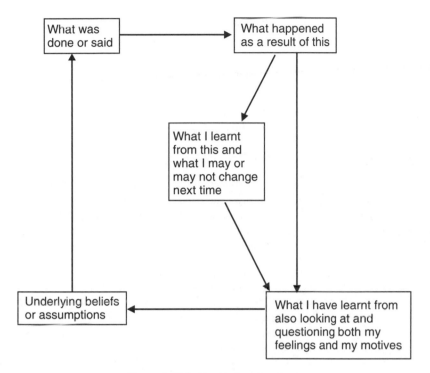

Figure 1.1(b) 'Double loop learning'.

To explain – when we do or say something, there are or will be consequences. If we carry out a basic evaluation similar to that described in Figure 1.1(a), we are undertaking what Argyris and Schon describe as 'single loop learning'. By so doing however, we could be also making the assumption that our thoughts, actions and feelings are already justifiable, so if something unexpected happens, we don't rethink our own position, but try and make conclusions that fit our current standpoint.

If on the other hand (see Figure 1.1(b)), we actively question both our feelings and our motives for doing and speaking as we did, we undertake 'double loop learning' – we look at the wider context and we question what our underlying beliefs, attitudes and values are that make us act, think and feel the way we do. Double loop learning doesn't assume we are already 'right' – it makes us face and examine the difference between 'espoused theory' (what we say to others that we know and believe) and 'theory-in-use' (what we actually do) (Argyris and Schon, 1974:6–7). In other words, this double loop learning model helps us objectively consider our practice by becoming aware of our simultaneous intuitive and subjective experience. This can greatly enlighten and change our practice.

There are a number of possible reflection 'points':

There is *reflection in action* – stop and think while in process, use intuition etc.
There is *reflection on action* – thinking after the event.
There is *reflection on inaction* – thinking about what I (or others) didn't do and why.
There is *reflection before action* – thinking in advance, visualizing how it might be etc.

We can illustrate all of these when thinking about a particular incident or experience.

Reflection – Ali

I had taken some cargo nets down to a local new adventure playground and the children decided they wanted a hammock strung up between the climbing frame and the metal fence and asked for my help. They wanted it quite high up and I asked them what they thought might happen if they fell out of it or it broke. They agreed to come lower. I also said that it would be good to start with only one person at a time – I found myself making an executive decision and telling them this rather than suggesting it. Why (reflection in action)? That wasn't my normal style. So I asked if they agreed, explaining why (the nets were a rather unknown factor in terms of strength) and they said okay. We eventually got the hammock tied up – I had to do all the knots as they didn't know how and I showed those who were interested in knowing, how to do them. Play ensued. I found myself uneasy about leaving them to it and so didn't – I also repeated the 'rule' of only one at a time on a few occasions. After a very happy hour with me observing several play types during its use, the hammock finally gave way and ripped at one corner. We agreed it might be possible to mend, but the whole thing would have to come down first. Later I thought back on my uneasiness (reflection on action) – why was I so insistent? I decided that because there were quite a lot of children involved and many of them were not known to me, that I was just making a sensible risk assessment – after all there could potentially be a nasty injury if the net gave way (although when it did it went gracefully!). True enough, but when I dug a little deeper as to why I wasn't more trusting of the children's capabilities (reflection on inaction), I realized that my underlying thought was that 'if something happened, I would be responsible' and as I was just volunteering that day on a new playground where I had trained all the staff, I was over-reacting for fear of being found wanting and not having done and recorded a 'proper' risk assessment. I was surprised at how strong this fear and sense of responsibility was. I thought later that evening about what to do the next day (reflection before action) and as a result I talked to two or three of the staff about what had happened and what I felt and I also wrote up a hammock risk assessment which I showed to them. Two of us then mended the net and it got erected again that day (perhaps more wisely!) in a different spot with oversight by a different playworker.

Reflection opportunity

Can you identify the triggers in you that sometimes make you over-react in some play situations?

Reflection – Jacky

I remember working as a casual playworker and going for the first time to a playscheme that was held in the large yard belonging to some tenement flats, used as short-term sheltered accommodation for women and children who were the victims of domestic abuse. There was a large group of children, of all ages, waiting for the van and playworkers to arrive and obviously expecting 'something' to immediately be different when we did. However it was also clear that it was going to take some time for the 'something' to manifest itself; for the contents of the van to become available; for the very small playroom to be 'set up' and the only thing that was going to occur was mayhem. Luckily I had a pocket full of chalk that I had taken in order to have some way of breaking the ice (reflection before action) and quickly started doing a large rather silly drawing of myself on the concrete. Some of the children drifted over to see what I was doing and I put the rest of my chalk out on the ground. This was snatched up within seconds and so I immediately went to see if there was any more in the playroom (reflection in action). Luckily there was, including some giant chalks which I gave to the youngest children. The yard floor soon became a wonderful colourful mural with pictures and graffiti and all sorts (some not very acceptable but also not destined to last very long) and a good half hour went by during which time the other two playworkers were able to make a great deal more play materials available. Thinking later, I realized (reflection after the event) that if children are to have a sense of ownership in relation to their play environment they must be given the opportunity to 'open up' the facility and 'unload' mobile play vans otherwise in some circumstances there will always be these periods of time when time has to be filled or trouble may break out because expectant children become bored. I realize that this is not always easy to organize due to working hours, availability of venue or resources etc., and (reflection on inaction) this was the case in this particular scenario. Whenever possible the organization should involve the children. However I also realized that in case time does have to be filled, it is always a good idea for playworkers to have 'something up their sleeves' and I now always ensure that I have a source of immediate possibilities for play available. Cards and magic tricks (particularly ones involving your own body) can be useful; juggling balls, skipping ropes and marbles can pass some time; occasionally, if you are outgoing, singing silly songs or speaking silly rhymes goes down well. Each of us has our own potential for ideas that will fit different situations and different types of children.

Reflection opportunity

What ideas do you have for different types of instant play, when time needs to be filled? Can you think of ideas that would suit children of all ages, genders and differing play needs?

Reflection in these terms does require commitment, self-awareness, openness and willingness to 'move beyond' and 'think outside of the box'. It can be both uncomfortable and powerful because it always seeks to know why and to understand a wide range of perspectives and motives.

We will each have our difficulties with it.

1 Making and taking the time
2 Being really honest
3 Digging deep enough

4 Fear of finding out or being found out
5 Lack of support or understanding by others
6 It may well mean change
7 Clarifying what to actually reflect on, how and why
8 Making it personally meaningful as opposed to doing what is required
9 Finding ways of doing it that suit me.

Reflection opportunity

How reflective are you? How often do you question why you do what you do and what the impact is of your feelings? If for example certain behaviours of children wind you up or make you anxious, do you consider why that is or do you 'blame' the child?

There are a number of areas and questions we can focus on to encourage us to reflect. We give a selection of these below and encourage you to start asking and thinking!

Reflection opportunity

1 *Thinking about what I did and felt when I played and the relevance this may have.* For example are my experiences the same or different to others – both then and now? How do my experiences affect my attitudes to children now? How do my experiences impact on my interaction with children now? Do I try to inhibit or recreate any of my experiences? Am I still 'playing out' some of the feelings and issues I had then? . . .

2 *Thinking about my interactions and interventions with children.* For example what feelings do I experience when watching children playing and why? What behaviours trigger fear, anxiety, anger, frustration, excitement, sadness . . . in me? How do I block or inhibit play? When do I get too involved, too directive, too instructive . . .? Why did I just say or do that?

3 *Observing children playing now and thinking about how this can inform my understanding and improve my practice.* For example what are they playing and how – what with, who with and where? How does it change? How does it end? What feelings are evident? What play types are being displayed? What cues are being given out, what returns are going on, what play frames and narratives are happening and who or what is creating them? How does age, gender, culture impact on playing?

4 *Observing the physical play environment and thinking about how this supports or inhibits play.* For example what different kinds of spaces exist – can/do these change? What is new and stimulating? What resources or materials have high play value? Is there play with the elements? Are there nooks and crannies and diverse-shaped spaces? Which areas attract children – where do children spend most of their time and why?

5 *Observing the affective play environment and thinking about how this supports or inhibits play.* For example what kinds of lighting are there? What colours are about? What kinds of music are played? What smells are around? What feelings are stimulated by or expressed in different spaces? What

unwritten rules exist and who made them? Are children supported in freely expressing their emotions?

6 *Observing other adults in a play environment.* For example are they observant, responsive, supportive or are they directive, prescriptive, inflexible? Are they playful and permissive, or fearful and controlling? What messages – verbally and non-verbally are they giving out? What are they actually doing and what impact does this have on children and their playing?

7 *Reading relevant literature and thinking critically about how this informs or relates to practice.* For example can I see this happening? What other evidence bears this out? Does this relate to my past and/or present experience? What does my intuition say about this? . . .

Reflective practice in playwork is essential because we have a supportive and responsive role to a myriad of unique individuals who are spontaneously playing out their emotions, thoughts and fantasies. Only careful and honest thinking by playworkers will lead us to understanding how to best attend to them.

We will look at different examples of reflecting as we go along and we will be posing questions here and there in each chapter. But first – a closer look at play itself.

Further reading

Gibbs, G. (1988) *Learning by Doing: A Guide to Teaching and Learning Methods.* London: Further Education Unit.

Hughes, B. (2001) *Evolutionary Playwork and Reflective Analytic Practice.* London: Routledge.

Palmer, S. (2003) 'Reflective Practice' in Brown, F. *Playwork – Theory & Practice.* Buckingham: Open University Press.

References

www.infed.org/thinkers/argyris.htm

Argyris, C. and Schon, D. (1974) *Theory and Practice – Increasing Professional Effectiveness.* London: Jossey-Bass.

Benjamin, J. (1974) *Grounds for Play.* London: Bedford Square Press.

Daroon, W. (1977) 'Play' in *The Social World of the Child.* London: Jossey-Bass.

Hughes, B. (1996) *Play Environments: A Question of Quality.* London: Playlink.

Palmer, S. (2006) *Toxic Childhood.* London: Orion.

Russell, W. (2005) 'The Unnatural Art of Playwork: BRAWGS Continuum', in *Therapeutic Playwork Reader II.* Sheffield: Ludemos Associates.

Sutton-Smith, B. (1986) in Kelly-Byrne, D. (1989) *A Child's Play Life: An Ethnographic Study.* New York: Teachers College Press.

2 Play

An understanding of play is the basis of playwork. Without an honest attempt to appreciate play and all its perceived drives and manifestations, playworkers can only provide an impoverished version of playwork – one that does not recognize the vital importance of play in the life of a child – eat, sleep, breathe, defecate, play! In this chapter we will consider some of the meanings that are given to play by a range of theorists, including, more recently, playwork theorists. While reading this chapter it is important to keep in mind the influence that the playworker may have upon the playing life of a child, depending upon their understanding of play and their subsequent approach to providing for it. We cannot separate children and their play, but the meaning of play, as Sutton-Smith (1997) suggests, in his book *The Ambiguity of Play*, is indeed filled with 'ambiguity'. Play is an elusive concept and we can only give you an overview of it in this chapter, but we do signpost you to further reading material.

Play definitions and concepts

Play has been defined in a variety of ways that give it meaning, but for every concept or theory about play there is an alternative and seemingly contradictory view. Here are some simple examples in Figure 2.1.

It seems that play is in some way related to all areas of life as suggested by Guilbaud (2003:17) 'Play is a layer of living that can encompass all the subject areas and processes of living.'

Although play may be seen to be a somewhat slippery customer and much has been written and researched over the centuries about it by people in various disciplines, there has emerged from the playwork world, based on both previous theory and current practice, a

Figure 2.1 Opposing play definitions.

• Trivial – aimless activity	• Important – 'children's scientific research' Hughes (1996) in Best Play (2000)
• Complex – 'play as a lifelong simulation of the key neonatal characteristics of unrealistic optimism, egocentricity, and reactivity . . .' Sutton-Smith (1997:231)	• Simple – Take part in games for enjoyment Soanes et al. (2001:675)
• Cognitively developmental – play linked to intellectual growth and mastery of skills (Piaget)	• Physically developmental – leaping, jumping, running around and being physically active
• Imitative – copying the behaviour of others	• Revolutionary – creation of new ideas and things
• Predating culture – the forerunner of many of our rituals, philosophy and social mores (Huizinga)	• Developing culture – play that falls within the rules and norms of the child's existing culture
• Individual – 'Play is freely chosen, personally directed and intrinsically motivated' Play Wales (2005)	• Group activity – 'Much childhood social play is motivated more by a desire to be accepted by other children than by any special desire for freedom of play choice' Sutton-Smith (1999:241)
• Therapeutic – 'it is the act of playing that has the healing inherent in it' Sturrock et al. (1998:13)	• Harmful – playing about and causing annoyance or distraction to others or causing harm
• Positive – co-operative	• Negative – competitive
• Connected with safety – a means by which children learn to look after themselves and keep themselves safe	• Connected with danger – putting children at risk of serious injury or death because children often dare and push themselves to take almost life-threatening risks

general consensus about the manifestations, purposes and processes of play behaviour. A body of knowledge and an approach to that knowledge that is unique to playwork has been and is being developed and some of this has now been enshrined in playwork qualifications. For instance, The Playwork Principles as explained in Chapter 1 describe what is unique and valuable about play from a playwork perspective, such as; self-determination, positive affect for the individual and process not product. *Best Play* (2000) endorsed the Play Types and what constitutes a rich play environment, more fully described in Chapter 3, and these are widely accepted by different schools of thought. More of this body of evidence is contained in Chapter 3 – A New Paradigm for Play.

The following are some ideas about play that come from different eras and schools of thought but have informed and have relevance to, our current playwork thinking.

In her book, Garvey (1977:10) suggests the following as being generally acceptable characteristics of play:

1 Play is pleasurable, enjoyable, even when not actually accompanied by signs of mirth it is still positively valued by the player.
2 Play has no extrinsic goals. Its motivations are intrinsic and serve no other objectives. In fact it is more an enjoyment of means than an effort devoted to some particular end.

3 Play is spontaneous and voluntary. It is not obligatory but is freely chosen by the player.
4 Play involves some active engagement on the part of the player.
5 Play has certain systemic relations to what is not play.

Ellis (1973:123) suggests that 'children are playing when control of their behaviour is largely under their own control' and King (1988), Hughes (2001) and others used and updated these characteristics that developed into the definition that is now used in the Playwork Principles to describe play as 'freely chosen, personally directed and intrinsically motivated'. We would partly agree with this definition, but have some reservations as discussed later in the chapter.

Bruner (1989) suggested that the main characteristic of play is not its content, but its mode. 'Play is an approach to action, not a form of activity.' In other words it's not what you do but the way that you do it that makes it play. Guilbaud (2003:10) has further developed this idea of approach to action into 'a special way of being' and we (2007) have played with the idea that play is an 'Individual state that may involve thinking, feeling and/or doing, with anticipation of satisfaction (not necessarily fulfilled) whilst involved in the unnecessary.' This again puts play in the context of being a 'personal state of being or mind' rather than an activity or an approach to activity. It allows for the possibility that something can still be play even if pleasure is not experienced and nobody else can observe anything happening and that play is linked to emotion. For example, a child going over and over various versions of a close family member or friend dying in his mind, in order to come to terms with that sort of possibility and practise how he might feel or behave.

Groos (1989) quoted in Bruner et al. (1976:66) argued that 'Animals do not play because they are young, but they have their youth because they must play' thus emphasizing the role of play in development and as we shall see later in this chapter we see many continuing links between play and development. Indeed Brown (2008:8) sees the links between play and development as one of the fundamentals of playwork. 'Children learn and develop both while they are playing and through their play.'

Winnicott (1997) saw play as essentially creative and 'as if' behaviour and the links between play and creativity are reflected in much playwork practice and theory. Several of the currently accepted play types such as 'Imaginative Play' and 'Creative Play' reflect this. Else (2008:79) says that 'through play, children are driven to explore both material and imaginary worlds: they play with real objects and intangible concepts'.

Hughes (2002) thinks that play may act as 'an experiential filtering mechanism' so that potential experiences can first be encountered in a virtual, non-real way. This would support Sutton-Smith's (1997) notion that play is a way for the child to use up lots of brain function that otherwise would get lost and to try out things that otherwise would not get tried out. These links to the brain are further developed by Lester and Russell (2008:2) when they suggest that neuroscientific evidence implies that 'playing is a way of building and shaping the regions of the brain that concern emotion, motivation and reward, and developing a range of flexible responses across a number of adaptive systems that link the brain, the body and the social physical environment'.

Key question

Which of these resonate with any definitions that you have used to describe play?

Play theory

Over the years play has been variously described by adults and theorized to fit into any number of boxes on the basis of different scientific perspectives. This has led to different professional groups and policy makers having different understandings of play based on a range of anticipated outcomes fuelled by the scientific perspective that fits their organizational philosophy, funding criteria, etc. Play has thus been consciously or unconsciously 'used' to develop, improve, socialize, cure, educate, occupy, improve health of, entertain, relax, keep separate, or tire out, children.

There is a growing body of evidence and interest in children's play. Playworkers particularly have been and continue to be in a unique position to test out or interpret the practical application of the major play theorists and also to highlight the emergence of the body of knowledge that has been developed through evidence-based practice and articulated by playwork theorists. In recent years the focus on children's participation in decision making in social policy initiatives, such as Children's Fund work, has also helped to highlight the importance of play. Whenever children and their parents are asked about what is important to them, play is consistently given a high priority. With hindsight most adults also see their playing in childhood as powerfully significant and there is a vast amount of observational evidence that has been analysed to show that, no matter how much importance is given for time to play, children from all parts of the world and in all cultures play and play has an impact on their development. However one must beware of thinking that play is only about the future. It is not. Play's benefits are also firmly rooted in the here and now. Understanding of this notion is one of the main aspects that make playwork different from other disciplines working with children.

We have all had experience of playing and this in some ways shapes our views about play. Guilbaud (2003:17) puts it very nicely when she says 'We know the essence of play through the subjective experience of playing, but we are less able to know it through objective analysis and it is this dichotomy which is part of the essence of play'. We (2008) have written elsewhere that we also believe that the results of this subjective experience of play have a possible effect on the ways that male and female thinkers perceive play and playwork theory.

Photo 2.1 Creating Lego worlds.

Reflection opportunity

Are you aware of any differences in the way that male and female playworkers work with children? Have you ever reflected on your childhood memories of play with both male and female playworkers and if so are there any obvious differences? Do you think that your experience of playing as a boy or girl has had an effect on your perceptions of children's play now and if so what is that effect?

Sutton-Smith (1997) is one of the most modern thinkers about the subject of play who is not a playworker, but who is interested in play for its own sake. Unlike many other play theorists he does not give ownership of play to children alone. He goes some way to try and give due breadth to play, when he suggests that there are seven rhetorics (persuasive viewpoints) of play which are:

1 progress (primarily about development)
2 fate (destiny, magic, gambling, games of chance)
3 power (contest, conflict, status and heroics)

Photo 2.2 Girl with attitude.

4 identity (traditional and community celebrations in order to confirm, maintain or advance the identity of the community of players)
5 the imaginary (flexibility and creativity, inversion and irrationality)
6 the self (play related to the desirable experiences of the players – their satisfaction, such as fun, relaxation and escape)
7 frivolity (tricksters, playful protests against the order of the world, inversion of 'work ethic').

He gives validity to each of the seven rhetorics by giving them a historical background, a specific function and form and also recognizable players. He locates each within a particular discipline and names scholars who have done play-related research within that discipline. At the end of all his analysis, he suggests we can only see rhetorics as 'representing the possibility of a truth yet to be discovered'. He suggests we should think of play as 'adaptive variability' – that is, play as the means by which we learn to be adaptable. He states that Stephen Jay Gould, an eminent evolutionary biologist, suggests that humans need to possess characteristics usually devalued in society such as 'sloppiness', 'quirkiness', 'un-productability' and 'massive redundancy', and Sutton-Smith (1997) sees these as being the very processes that are developed through play and that make us flexible. The idea of flexibility is an important one in playwork so Brown (2003) talks about compound flexibility and Hughes (2001) talks about combinatorial flexibility.

Reflection – Jacky

My own understanding of play is probably based on a combination of the identity, imaginary, frivolity and self rhetorics. I like the idea of play subverting efforts of society to 'tame' us into good citizens, while helping us, through the opportunity for bizarre behaviour, to find ourselves and have fun with others. Much of the play that I have been personally involved in as a child or observed children involved in, when there are no adults in charge, is definitely anarchic – it is not the 'nice' play of 'turn taking', 'no breaking', 'calm making' that we see ruled over by adults, but the 'bear baiting', 'rule breaking' 'chaos creating' play of powerful animals! I see play as freedom.

Reflection – Ali

I look back at my childhood and see many examples of me playing that fit the rhetorics of power, fate and the imaginary. As the only girl playing with older brothers and their friends, my playing was a serious business and involved a lot of risk taking, competition and fantasy. For me, in those years play was definitely about survival!

Major play theories

In order to try and give some sort of coherence to the many play theories that abound we decided to locate a summary of some of the major ones into the quadrants of the Integral Play Framework model (Else 2004:17–20) (explained on page 37 in Chapter 3). This is intended to give a holistic overview, while also giving an indication of the variety of thinking related to play theory that has influenced our current theorizing. In each quadrant, we list first a few of the relevant play theorists over the last century. We then cite more recent playwork theorists who built on these play theories.

Reflection opportunity

Which of these relate to your experiences or thinking abut play?

Quadrant A – Myself: feelings and thoughts

Theories that fit into this category indicate that children's play is related to a child's emotions and intellect and is linked to development of the mind. Theories from this category are the basis of Play Therapy and Learning through Play. Theories, many suggested by Child (1985) in her paper on 'The General Theories of Play' that was commissioned by Playboard, a forerunner of Play England, as a government funded body for play, include:–

Psychoanalytic Theory	Freud (1907)
	Erikson (1965)

Behaviourist Learning Theory   Froebel (1826)
                                 Ellis (1973)
                                 Bruner (1971)
Cognitive Development Theory   Piaget (1951)

More recently as playwork theory

Psycholudics   Else and Sturrock (1998)

Quadrant B – My body: physical ability and skills

Theories that fit into this category indicate that children's play is linked to the development and adaptation of the human species. Theories from this category suggest variously that play reflects the history of man, that play is how children learn the skills to become independent and that play is linked to the survival of the fittest or of the species.

Recapitulation Theory   Hall (1920)
Practice Theory   Groos (1901)

More recently as playwork interpretation influenced by

Animal Play   Burghardt (2006)
Evolutionary Theory   Hughes (2001)

Quadrant C – Us: belief and culture

Theories that fit into this category indicate that children's play is linked to the development of culture and religion.

Play as culture   Huizinga (1949)
                                 Callois (1961)
                                 Dearden (1967)
Toys as culture   Sutton-Smith (1986)

More recently

Incorporating play in cultural   Playlink (2002)
strategies

Quadrant D – Our society: relationships, power and control

Theories that fit into this category indicate that children's play is linked to fitting a child into their society. Play enables children to learn the rules.

Socializing Theory	Plato and Aristotle
	Tinbergen (1975)
	Sutton-Smith (1979)
	Wohl (1974)
Communication Theory	Bateson (1972)

More recently there are further theories related to play

Gender Theory	Thorne (1993)
Group Socialization Theory	Rich-Harris (1998)
	Strandell (2000)

Playwork interpretation

| Play and social relationship skills | Rennie, S. (2003) |

A lot of theorizing for something that even children comment on by saying 'I was only playing'! So what has the play work sector made of all this?

Currently, although there are many and various views on play, there are three different paradigms of children's play based on current playwork theorists' ideas. These three paradigms incorporate three different schools of thought related to play, with different epistemological roots. Thus for the purposes of this chapter we have:

1 'Therapeutic Playwork Theory',
2 'Developmental Playwork Theory' and
3 'Evolutionary Playwork Theory'.

Each of these has a basis in theories that have been previously expounded, as above, and each has its proponents and antagonists. However there is a coalescing of some of these different schools of thought that forms enough common ground about the relationship of the play-worker with the process of playing that enables a constructive dialogue between the different proponents. This has led to the shared practical definition of play.

It is important to analyse the thinking behind each paradigm in order to inform your own thinking. Understanding of the scientific literature has contributed to playworkers' view of play and play like every other area of life is also influenced by the world around us and the current political, social and cultural mores of the time. In another era, another time, another place in the world, different viewpoints may be developed. Thinking is not static, like play it is changeable, quixotic and the stuff of life. Rennie (in Brown 2003:31) says that 'We work with a change process. If we do so with intent to practice professionally, we must show we can be as flexible as that process . . .' Indeed while there is common acceptance of the definition of play as 'freely chosen' etc. there is also awareness, through practice experience, that play can describe behaviour that is not freely chosen, that is negative and harmful. Sutton-Smith and

Kelly-Byrne (1984) describe play as 'often brutal and unpleasant' (p. 311) 'obscene and erotic' (p. 312) and 'children also use play to terrorize each other' (p. 313). Russell (2007) explores how playworkers should respond to freely chosen and self-directed play that disrupts the play of others, threatens safety or causes discomfort to adults. We as playworkers have to continue to develop our thinking in order to solve the incongruity of play with the real world.

Therapeutic playwork theory

Therapeutic playwork has grown out of the psychological theories of play. Freud was the first to recognize the therapeutic nature of play and later child psychotherapy was developed from this, based on the premise that play is a form of communication and transmission of emotions, unconscious experiences and thoughts. Carl Rogers explored the relationship between therapist and client and this idea is developed in Therapeutic Playwork Theory. In his paper 'The Sacred and the Profane Sturrock' (1995) he also explores the spiritual side of play. He cites Schiller's idea that the play impulse 'balances and reconciles the opposing thrusts of material and spiritual concerns' and this thread runs through much of Therapeutic Playwork Theory.

1 Freud's psychoanalytic theories are the basis for seeing play as potentially therapeutic. Freud considered that children often played to come to terms with unpleasant experiences and also that play was a sort of 'wish fulfillment' in that children could create their own world. Playing therefore helps with the development of self, identity and emotional well-being. In the words of Sturrock play is associated with 'being and becoming'.

2 Play has always been similar throughout the millennia and served the same purposes, namely to support 'the child's growing sense of self and identity, expression, meaning and content that develops emotional intelligence, the creation of social forms and emerging environmental consciousness' (Sturrock, 2002:1).

3 Play has both preventative and curative therapeutic value. Children often play in ways that enable them to experience emotions and feelings that they have not felt in real-life situations. This experimentation may well help them to better cope with difficult emotions and feelings if and when they come along. It is also through play that a child can play out some of his or her actual experiences that may cause psychological difficulties, later in life, if not dealt with at the time.

4 The modern environment has become less suitable for play that has in turn increased the need for adult involvement. This involvement has led to adults instead of children being in charge of the play and also these adults may consciously or unconsciously 'contaminate' the play by seeing it from an adult perspective rather than a child's.

5 A playwork setting should be one in which the child has trust in – the place, the people in it and where the workers understand how children express themselves during play. 'The playground in practice becomes "the locus of self-ordinated healing by the children" a setting where the child can have "safe emergencies"' Sturrock (2002:4).

6 An important part of a therapeutic playworker's role is to be able to recognize and have strategies for dealing with their own un-played-out material in the playspace so that they can be in service of the child's own healing process. Un-played-out material refers to those experiences and perspectives from our own history that can obstruct or contaminate our perceptions now.

7 The playworker and the child both change and develop through playing, the playworker consciously and the child unconsciously, and thus the play situation is a constantly changing one that requires ongoing analysis by the playworker. The relationship between child/ren and playworker has similarities to that of a therapist and client.

Reflection opportunity

Does this resonate for you? Are you aware of children using their play to make sense of their lives? Do you seek ways to support this?

We have certainly witnessed many children when they are playing having 'safe emergencies'. We have seen many children or their toys 'dying' over and over again and I have seen 'funerals' being enacted. We have seen 'planes, trains and cars crashing', 'operations being undertaken or endured'. Indeed we have had many of these 'operations' performed on ourselves and we have 'died' and been 'resurrected' as we imagine have many of you in the name of play. We have seen children (or 'animals') 'becoming lost and not being found', or 'running away and going to new homes'. We have seen children being 'chased by monsters' and having to

Photo 2.3 In his own world.

'fight and overcome' them. When they are playing we have seen children willingly 'submitting themselves to almost unendurable fright' by summoning up 'ghosts and ghouls'. We have seen children 'making war' and we have seen children being victorious and being defeated in a myriad of ways during play. We have also seen children participating in 'domestic dramas' and pretending to be 'lonely, unhappy, sick, in pain' and many, many more states of being. Sometimes as adults we have wanted to manipulate that play to make it all turn out well, but our playwork knowledge has enabled us to let the 'bad times roll'.

Developmental playwork theory

Many people, who theorized about play, found some form of link between play and human development whether that is physical, emotional, mental or social.

During the eighteenth and nineteenth centuries play was largely seen as an alternative to work for children and a chance to get rid of excess energy. Many classical theorists of the nineteenth and early twentieth century tried to link play to human development but their ideas were mainly based on philosophy and informal observation rather than rigorous research.

Most children pass through recognizable developmental milestones at particular stages of life (e.g. smiling, eruption of teeth, walking, talking, reading etc.) and these can be monitored through observation, testing and measuring. Information gained from a range of different disciplines such as psychology, philosophy, biology, anthropology, sociology and education, has been used to support the notion that play is related to this child development.

1 Piaget, a developmental psychologist, observed children playing and discovered that different types of play appeared at different stages and ages and his theories dominated thought on the nature of children's thinking and learning during the 1960s and 1970s.
2 Educational pioneers such as Froebel, Montessori and Isaacs recognized that play is an essential medium for mastery of skills, learning and development and introduced play into education.
3 Vygotsky, a Russian psychologist, who saw learning as a social experience, believed that play helps children to understand the function of symbols which in turn helps with language and literacy development.
4 Groos, a biologist, saw play as highly purposeful and as an indispensable agent of growth. In order for development of instincts and impulses to fully mature he thought that they had to be 'pre-exercised' through play in childhood.
5 Young, a zoologist and, more recently, other neurobiologists have advanced biological theories in relation to play and the way it helps the immature brain of a child to develop to its full capability. Babies are born with a full complement of nerve cells but these are immature and do not connect up. If the brain cells are not used they will be lost. Play is a way of enabling children to use their brain cells when other experiences may not be available to them.
6 Play is also seen as very important in the development of social skills. According to Hendricks (2001:51) this notion was originally based on a study carried out by M. Parten in 1932 that identified the development of stages of social playing in young children from solitary to co-operative play.

As a result of all the above, and although it was never a description of play, in the mid-1980s, the acronym SPICE began to be used (sometimes inappropriately) by some playwork trainers, as an 'aide memoire' to think about how playwork could provide for specific areas of child development by offering: Social interaction; Physical activity; Intellectual stimulation; Creative achievement and Emotional stability. However this led, in some instances, to an overemphasis on the developmental nature of play, which in turn led to over-structured ways of planning for play that took little account of the wealth of other theories that support the importance of free play.

Brown (2003:53–63) explains that SPICE was part of a theoretical construct of 'compound flexibility' that demonstrated that a flexible environment and atmosphere can lead to development of self-confidence, self-awareness and self-acceptance which in turn leads to the development of flexibility within the child and therefore the ability to cope with an ever-changing world. This explanation supported the notion that play could not be planned to lead to specific areas of development.

It can be seen that there are many ways of linking play to child development. However during the latter part of the twentieth and early part of the twenty-first century, the emphasis has been particularly on the educational and socializing aspects of play almost to the exclusion of other areas of development. This has resulted in play being used as a tool for

Photo 2.4 What's out there?

development of those things that adults wish children to develop and been adopted by edu-cationalists and early years workers almost to the exclusion of other possible 'non-beneficial to society' but 'beneficial to children and their culture' benefits that play may support. Some current playwork practice has been influenced by this imbalance. There is a danger that with-out a full understanding of play, that playworkers can be overly influenced by these more dominant rhetorics. We need to realize that if we try to predetermine the outcome of play, we can destroy the very thing that makes it play.

Reflection – Ali

I remember visiting an after-school club where a worker was sitting at a table with several children who were all making cards from a pile of materials the worker had provided. The worker said she wanted to 'promote their creative and social development through play'. After about 20 minutes one child stood up the card she had made on the table and said to the worker 'can I go and play now?' The worker said of course she could – but wasn't making the card playing too? The child looked at the worker with that look of the ancients that children often display and said gently 'no – I was doing it because you wanted me to'. . . .

Key question

Have you 'oversubscribed' to the developmental rhetoric? Do you think we can encourage children's development by deciding in advance what they should do and how?

Evolutionary playwork theory

Evolutionary playwork has its basis in some of the early classical theories about play that are based around biological and physiological reasons why children play. Much of this thought stemmed from Darwin's 'Origin of the Species'. Links to animal play are still important in Evolutionary Playwork Theory.

'Play, the behavioural and psychic equivalent of oxygen' Hughes (2000) and 'a vitally important ingredient in the development and evolution process' Hughes (2001:8–9).

1 Groos as summarized in Child (1985:3) particularly viewed play as an impulse to practise instinctual, inherited behaviour necessary for survival.
2 Hall's recapitulation theory indicated links to instincts and heredity but saw play as going through the evolutionary stages that man had gone through from prehistoric to modern times. Thus as children develop they go through animal, savage, nomad, planter and tribal stages of play.
3 The psychologist, Wilber develops Hall's theme and suggests that the stages of play might be in terms of an evolving consciousness. 'Play enables humans to feel "at ease" with their situation.' Hughes summarizing Wilber (1996) (2001:118).

4 Hughes' (2001:8–9), theories are based in evolutionary psychology (a fusion of cognitive psychology and evolutionary biology) sees play as being a 'vitally important ingredient in the development and evolution process'. In its crudest sense he believes that children's play is linked to the very survival of our species.

5 Hughes (2001:118) contends that

> play has evolved as a biological mechanism to enable human beings to come to terms with what and where they are and have some control over and understanding of what is happening to them. That through their playful interactions with their physical and psychological environments, they develop an individual and collective relationship with these environments which enables them to make some sense of human existence.

6 Interestingly whereas Brown's description of 'compound flexibility' is part of the developmental paradigm (see above), Hughes interpretation of 'combinatorial flexibility' is drawn from the biological sciences notably from Kathy Sylva (1977). She suggests that 'play trains the animal (or child) to string bits of behaviour together to form novel solutions to problems'.

7 More recently Hughes has been influenced by the work of people in the area of animal play for example Burghardt (2006:82) who sees play as 'repeated, incompletely functional behaviour differing from more serious versions structurally, contextually, or ontogenetically, and initiated voluntarily when the animal is in a relaxed or low stressed state'.

8 Evolutionary playworkers believe in the need for children to have opportunities to play in 'adult free' environments or with very limited adult intervention. They think that playwork is about modifying the environment for play in order to redress an imbalance in lack of opportunity for children to play with the elements, take risks and play freely. (Play is categorized into types and features intrinsic to individual development, species adaptation and evolution.)

9 Hughes believes that the result, over time, of play deprivation (no opportunity for children to play freely and take risks in a rich and elemental environment free from adulteration) is that our children may not be able to adapt and evolve naturally and that that in turn will endanger the survival of human kind as a species.

Evolutionary theories related to play make the role of a playworker vital in today's constrained Western world where most of a child's time is spent in organized and educational activity or in an uncreative environment where passive entertainment is the norm.

Reflection opportunity

Do the concepts of evolutionary playwork make sense of what you think and feel about playing – whether in your own experience or that of children playing now?

Reflection – Jacky

I have recently become very aware, by playing with my grandchildren, just how children string together different ideas, or behaviour, in a very flexible way and use this adaptability to find solutions to problems.

Photo 2.5 Night rider.

> They do not have to stay within reality in the way that adults do, but see the possibilities in everything. A fine example when I was playing the game 'Hic Hac Hoc' or as my grandson calls it 'Paper, Scissors, Stone' is that if I won, he would simply suggest a new item that could beat mine. So for instance if he said 'Stone' and I said 'I have Paper and it can wrap your Stone up'. He would say 'But I have "Fire" so I can burn your "Paper"'. So if I then said 'But I have "Water" and can put your "Fire" out', he would say 'But I have a "Plug" and I can pull it out and let all the water out. Ha Ha beat that Granny!'

So here we have it – three different ways of looking at playwork, but remarkably proponents of each do not disregard the others. Though the playwork sector continues to debate, argue, research and theorize, there is still considerable consensus about the purposes of playing and the consequent role of the playworker, much of which has been enshrined in the Playwork Principles.

While we have been writing this chapter, Lester and Russell (2008) have consolidated the emerging body of evidence based on our current understandings and interpretations of play. From their major review of published literature about play across all disciplines, they take some key messages and these include the belief that play affects 'the architectural foundations of development' such as the very way that our brains develop and the way that our genes are expressed. They also suggest that 'play makes a major contribution to developing emotion regulation', thus helping to build a child's resilience. Their findings support the notion that play should be provided for its own sake and that 'play provision should be judged on whether it enables children to play rather than on more instrumental outcomes'.

Key questions

So which of the following seems to encapsulate for you why human children play?

1 They will learn and practise the competencies they need.
2 They will develop their thinking and problem-solving processes.
3 Their brains will make the necessary synaptic connections for healthy growth.
4 They will master a whole range of feelings they encompass and experience.
5 They will continue to evolve and enable the ongoing existence of our species.
6 They pass on customs and cultures and create new ones.
7 They adapt, invent and explore – all necessary skills for survival.
8 They find ways to communicate and thus acquire empathy and social skills.
9 They ask and come to terms with questions around life, death, immortality and morality.
10 They discover who and what they and others are.
11 They will find out and try out their increasing strengths and capabilities.
12 They learn to regulate their emotions and become resilient.
13 They seek out novelty and uncertainty to test their responses.
14 They can be daft, silly, nonsensical.
15 They can express their 'darker side'.
16 They just have to!

The literary evidence, the observations made by playworkers, the current and ongoing research into play indicates strongly that all of these take place. Play is indeed multifaceted and its ultimate function for humankind is to maintain our adaptability, vigour and optimism in the face of an uncertain, risky and demanding world" (Kane, 2004:63).

In this chapter we have given an overview of some of the thinking on play that abounds, with particular emphasis on the play theories that influence the playwork world. In Chapter 3 we outline the results of this influence by explaining some of the finer points of playing. We hope we have provoked your own thinking and feeling about play and that you will not stop here!

Is our society ready to see play as a universal right for children regardless of whether it achieves tangible outcomes? At this point 23 November 2008, this has not been the case, but we have the greatest of hopes that by the time this book is published, there may be a greater understanding of the importance of play for play's sake.

Further reading

Abrams, R. (1997) *The Playful Self*. London: Fourth Estate.

Brown, F. (Ed.) (2003) *Playwork Theory and Practice*. Buckingham: Open University Press.

Brown, F. and Cheesman, B. (2003) 'Introduction: Childhood and Play' in F. Brown (Ed.), *Playwork Theory and Practice*. Buckingham/ Philadelphia: Open University Press.

Davey, A. and Gallagher, J. (2006) *New Playwork: Play and Care for Children 4–16*. London: Thomson Learning.

Else, P. (2009) *The Value of Play* Continuum London.

Hughes, B. (2001) *Evolutionary Playwork and Reflective Analytic Practice.* Routledge: London.

Huizinga, J. (1955) *Homo Ludens a Study of the Play Element in Culture.* Boston: Beacon Press.

Lester, S. and Russell, W. (2008) *Play for a Change.* London: National Children's Bureau.

Sturrock, G., Russell, W. and Else, P. (2004) *Towards Ludogogy Parts 1, 11 and 111.* Sheffield: Ludemos.

Sutton-Smith, B. (1997) *The Ambiguity of Play.* Cambridge, MA: Harvard University Press.

References

Brown, F. (2003) 'Compound Flexibility: The Role of Playwork in Child Development' in F. Brown (Ed.) *Playwork Theory and Practice.* Buckingham/Philadelphia: Open University Press.

Brown, F. (2008) 'The Fundamentals of Playwork' in *Foundations of Playwork.* Eds. Fraser Brown and Chris Taylor. Maidenhead: McGraw-Hill Open University Press.

Bruner, J. S., Jolly, A. and Sylva, K. (1976) *Play, Its Role in Development and Evolution.* Harmondsworth, Middx.: Penguin.

Burghardt, G. (2006) *The Genesis of Animal Play: Testing the Limits.* Cambridge, Mass.: MIT.

Child, E. (1985) *General Theories of Play.* Birmingham, UK: Playboard.

Crowe, B. (1983) *Play is a Feeling.* London, UK: George Allen & Unwin.

Ellis, M. (1973) *Why People Play.* New Jersey: Prentice Hall.

Else, P. (2008:81) 'Playing: The Space Between' in *Foundations of Playwork.* Eds. Fraser Brown and Chris Taylor. Maidenhead: McGraw-Hill Open University Press.

Garvey, C. (1977) *Play. The Developing Child.* London: Fontana/Open Books and Open Books Publishing Limited.

Guilbaud, S. (2003) 'The Essence of Play' in F. Brown (Ed.) *Playwork Theory and Practice.* Buckingham/Philadelphia: Open University Press:

Harris, J. R. (1998) *The Nurture Assumption.* London: Bloomsbury.

Hendricks, B. E. (2001) *Designing For Play.* Ashgate: England.

Henrig, R. M. quoting Bekoff, M. (2008) 'Taking Play Seriously' in *The New York Times Magazine.*

Hughes (1996) in NPFA (2000) *Best Play What Play Provision Should Do for Children.* NPFA, London: Children's Play Council and Playlink.

Hughes, B. (2001) *Evolutionary Playwork and Reflective Analytic Practice.* London: Routledge.

Kane, P. (2004) *The Play Ethic.* London: Macmillan.

King, F. (1988) The Right to Play towards a policy for children's play in Bristol. Unpublished discussion paper.

Lester, S. and Russell, W. (2008) *Play for a Change.* London: National Children's Bureau.

Lester, S. and Russell, W. (2008) *Preview: Play for a Change.* London: Play England.

Play Wales (2005) *Playwork Principles* (online) Cardiff: Play Wales. Available from http://www.playwales.org.uk/page.asp?id=50

Playlink (2002) *Play as Culture Incorporating Play in Cultural Strategies.* CPPF, Children's Play Council, DCMS, DTLR and Dept. for Education and Skills.

Rennie, S. (2003), Making Play Work: The Fundamental Role of Play in the Development of Social Relationship Skills. In *Playwork Theory and Practice.* Ed. Fraser Brown. Buckingham: Open University Press.

Rich-Harris J. (1998) *The Nurture Assumption.* New York: Touchstone.

Russell, W. (2007) *Reframing Playwork: Reframing Challenging Behaviour.* Nottingham: City of Nottingham.

Soanes, C. Spooner, A. and Hawker, S. (Eds) (2001) *Oxford Paperback Dictionary Thesaurus & Wordpower Guide.* New York: Oxford University Press Inc.

Sturrock, G. (1995) *The Sacred and The Profane*. Sheffield: Ludemos Associates.

Sturrock, G. (2002) *The Idea of Unplayed Out Material*. Sheffield: Ludemos Associates/BITP.

Sturrock, G. and Else, P. (1998) 'The Playground as Therapeutic Space: Playwork as Healing', known as *The Colorado Paper*. Sheffield: Ludemos.

Sturrock, G., Russell, W. and Else P. (2004) *Towards Ludogogy Parts 1, 11 and 111: The Art of Becoming Through Play*. Sheffield: Ludemos.

Sutton-Smith, B. (1997) *The Ambiguity of Play*. Cambridge, MA: Harvard University Press.

Sutton-Smith, B. (1999) 'Evolving a Consilience of Play Definitions: Playfully', in *Play and Culture Studies 2*, 239–56.

Sutton-Smith, B. and Kelly-Byrne, D. (1984) 'The Idealization of Play' in Smith, P. *Play in Animals and Humans*. Oxford: Basil Blackwell.

Sylva, K. (1977) 'Play and Learning' in Tizard, B. and Harvey, D. (Eds) *Biology of Play*. London: Heinemann.

Taylor, C. (1998) 'Why Good Enough Is Good Enough', in *Playwords*, 7, 12–13. Common Threads.

Thorne, B. (1993) *Gender Play: Girls and Boys in School*. New Brunswick NJ: Rutgers University Press.

Winnicott, D. (1997) *Playing and Reality*. London: Routledge.

Wood, A. and Kilvington, J. (2008), Personal communication.

A New Paradigm for Play   3

Professionalizing playwork

In the last chapter we considered a variety of theories around play both old and new. This chapter takes a look at the consequent theoretical information that has built up within playwork and that now informs the repertoire of interventions into children's play that many experienced playworkers make. There is also a growing confidence and articulation for these ideas within the wider playwork world. They have started to underpin the professionalization of playwork through training and quality assurance schemes (see also Chapter 9).

There is sometimes a tension between playwork theorists and practitioners in relation to their ideas about play and how to provide for it. How play is viewed by the playwork world is, as said before, like most aspects of life, affected by social and political factors (see Chapter 8). In the current era many of the playworkers who staff much of what purports to be playwork, that is, care schemes such as after-school clubs and holiday play care schemes for children of school age, have been legally obligated to undertake NVQs at levels 2 or 3 (or their vocational equivalents) of either playwork or Early Years. While this has in many ways potentially led to a 'professionalizing' of the work it has also, in some people's view, led to a 'dumbing down' of the knowledge base of playworkers because little current play and playwork theory was previously embedded in the standards.

SkillsActive is the Sector Skills Council for Playwork and currently oversees all playwork training and education. It has developed a UK Strategy for Playwork Education, Training and Qualifications lasting from 2006 to 2011. It has a vision to build a professional workforce 'with appropriate professional skills and competences to support children's play' (2006:18). The latest NVQs Levels 2 and 3 and 4 in playwork (and their vocational equivalents), already reflect this need for more up-to-date theoretical underpinning of performance and combine much current playwork theory, with its practical application. The intention is to create a stronger knowledge base for the work of those people undertaking these new awards which should in turn create better and more obvious routes into Higher Education thus potentially increasing the numbers of people researching into play and playwork, thereby nourishing the sector.

Interestingly we remember a time when few playworkers were obligated to undertake any form of training. They learnt playwork by doing it and some playworkers still feel that this is the way that playwork skills can best be developed. When NVQs came in many playworkers felt that it was 'a step too far' fearing that the very processes that had to be gone through to prove competence were actually deskilling them. Some playworkers prefer to learn the theory without having to demonstrate how to put it into practice while others feel competent in the practical aspects of playwork but find it difficult to relate the theory to practice.

> ## Key question
>
> What are your views?

The model for play, at this time, is mainly influenced by evolutionary, therapeutic and developmental play theory and based on the assumption, as previously discussed, that 'Children's play is freely chosen, personally directed behaviour and motivated from within'. Play is thus seen as an essential and innate process and a necessity for the biological, psychological and social well-being and healthy development and survival of children, which in turn informs the role of the playworker. (See Chapter 1 for details.)

Some of the concepts from evolutionary, therapeutic and developmental theories for play are elaborated below and are essential knowledge for the reflective playwork approach. There is also the inclusion of some sociological theory here. Currently this does not feature as significantly in the widely accepted theoretical construct of playwork, perhaps through the fear that the involvement of a playworker with a child might be seen as a socializing relationship with the playworker 'bringing the child on' to be a co-operative member of society, when in actuality the purpose of the interface between playworker and child is play. This 'interface' is discussed further in this chapter.

The randomness of children's play behaviour can sometimes make it difficult for us to see how play affects the whole child. We often break the affect up into a range of different areas in order to simplify our thoughts. The following is an attempt to show how a child develops his or her whole self through play.

Play framework

A framework is a supporting or underlying structure and within any discipline a visual framework can be a useful tool for showing how ideas and theories are linked. The Integral Play Framework 2004:17–20, gives us a way of looking at the world from a holistic viewpoint and when focusing on the elements of developmental play shows how our feelings and thoughts (psychological and cognitive development), physical ability and skills (physiologi-

Figure 3.1 Integral play framework 1.
Source: Taken from 'The integral play framework' Tables 1 and 2 in *Towards Ludogogy Part 1* Sturrock, Russell and Else (2004)

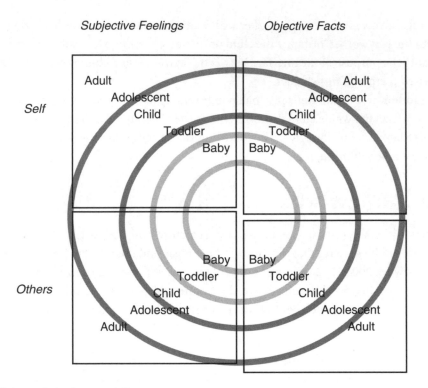

Subjective Feelings — Objective Facts

Self

Adult
Adolescent
Child
Toddler
Baby

Adult
Adolescent
Child
Toddler
Baby

Others

Baby
Toddler
Child
Adolescent
Adult

Baby
Toddler
Child
Adolescent
Adult

Figure 3.2 Integral play framework 2.
Source: Taken from 'The integral play framework' Table 3 in *Towards Ludogogy Part 1* Sturrock, Russell and Else (2004)

cal development), beliefs and culture (cultural development) and our relationships, power and control (social and political development) develop alongside each other and how areas of our experience overlap.

During their play children will flexibly move between various modes, using their bodies, voices, relationships, rules, imitations, jokes etc. in a random yet integral way thereby developing their sense of self within their own environment and milieu. 'If I feel/think this, then do that, what happens?' 'If I do this and that happens, what do I think or feel about it?' (2004:19) and what do others think and feel about what I have done and do they know how I feel? All of this is assimilated into the child's mind and over time is accommodated to form part of the child's sense of self and skill base. The process continues on throughout life.

So when children are randomly playing they are developing themselves. But how does the actual play process occur? How does it get started? How does it keep itself going? What makes it stop? How do we know when or how to respond to it? What does it look like? How do we know if a child is playing? The following sections are an attempt to explain some of this.

Play frame

A frame is a boundary or a surround for something. The play frame can be a material or non-material boundary (a place in the environment or in the mind or emotions) that contains play episodes that can last from moments to weeks or months, for example, two children playing at 'house' in a den – the den is the material frame; a child daydreaming – the edges of the fantasy are the non-material frame; a child pretending to throw a hand grenade to cue the start of an ongoing game of war – a narrative frame with the narrative containing the play over what might be a substantial period of time.

Reflection – Jacky

As a young girl I remember playing at 'horses' with a small group of girl friends (we never played with boys!). This game happened during most playtimes at school over at least one term. We each had our horse and rider name and each of us had obtained either rope or old baby reigns with which to 'harness' and control our horse, when we were the riders. We sometimes made rosettes, used jumpers as horse blankets, and had gymkhanas and races. We designated a certain part of the playground as the stables, paddocks etc. (these places were often, also being used by other children for other purposes which required negotiation or argument to sort out) where we horses or riders would sleep, be groomed, exercised etc. Often no actual decision about who would be horse or rider was made, it just happened at the designated place at playtime. We would get into pairs (or be a lone horse that just galloped around on their own and tried to join in) and the narrative would continue from the previous playtime or would be altered as we went along by changes in behaviour. For example a horse might suddenly decide to rear up and 'throw' its rider who would cry for help and then might die, be ignored or be ministered to with first aid. Sometimes instructions might be issued from one player or discussions might be had about who was treating their horse well or badly; whether it was night time or a gymkhana; if an adventure such as a 'baddy' coming to steal a horse was about to ensue etc. Sometimes the discussion was the only thing that happened. All this occurred in a random, opposing and ongoing basis. The playing was chaotic and exciting. I remember dreaming about the game and looking forward to it with an intensity I never felt about anything else to do with school at the time.

A play frame provides the context for play and is chosen and initiated by the child. It is important that the playworker knows how to recognize and 'contain' these frames while holding the integrity of the play (not trying to change it so that it better fits their idea of what play should be). On rare occasions it may be necessary to gently reframe play when it seems that the child or children have become stuck, or maybe one frame is dominating, for example, a football game in a small school yard, but this can all too easily slip over into trying to create what the adult considers to be more appropriate play frames thereby dominating and adulterating play and robbing it of its 'self-ordinated' developmental or healing potential, that is, the child's own internal developmental and healing mechanism.

A play frame can be demonstrated in the following way and can be used as a tool to reflect upon ways of improving the environment; resources or interventions, to extend or support particular children's play (see also diagrams in the section on the Play Process below).

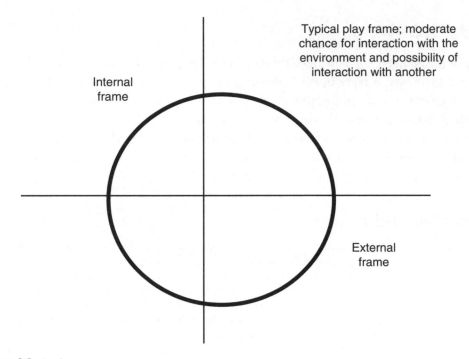

Typical play frame; moderate chance for interaction with the environment and possibility of interaction with another

Internal frame

External frame

Figure 3.3 Play frame.
Source: Taken from 'The Playground as therapeutic space: playwork as healing'. Else and Sturrock (1998)

The play cycle

A cycle is a series of events that are regularly repeated or a complete sequence of changes with an associated recurring phenomenon. Through observation or through reflection we must all be aware of the cyclic nature of play, for example, hide your face behind something and pop up and say 'boo' and a small child will repeatedly chuckle with glee. Those people who have studied psycholudics (the study of the mind or psyche at play) have developed a model of The Play Cycle. This is a formula to describe the process of play, within a play frame, by which a child is motivated to play, plays and then stops playing. The concepts within The Play Cycle can be very useful in helping playworkers to better facilitate the play process. Although some of these concepts can at first seem complex it is worth persevering with them as they will bring about a heightened understanding of play and therefore a better understanding of the playwork role.

For the purposes of description the cycle, which occurs within the play frame, has been given four functional components:

1 The metalude or the part of the mind where the drive or 'cue' to play is issued – the motivation to play. A play cue is an action that invites play – it may be simple such as a verbal request. It may be subtle such as a slight change in facial expression or it may be complex such as setting up a complicated game and not appearing to do anything further. The idea would be that the game is a 'lure' to others to play, however the child simply waits.

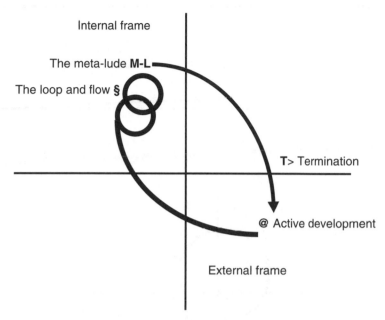

Figure 3.4 The Play cycle.
Source: Adapted from The ludic feedback cycle in 'The Playground as therapeutic space: playwork as healing'.
Else and Sturrock (1998)

2 Termination or decay; the breakdown of the drive to play over time – lessening of motivation. Play can wane and stop in a matter of moments or over days. Who has not seen children engaged in a new craze that goes on and on and then suddenly disappears or gradually fades away.

3 The play return – the response to the play cue which develops the action from either, the mind, the environment or other player. Without a satisfactory return the playing will never get going. Some children (it is suggested particularly children with ADHD) do not cue effectively and they become frustrated because their cues are ignored by others or their mind does not become sufficiently taken up with the possibilities of play.

4 The loop and flow – the processing of the play return within the metalude which may set up a flow of play so that the playing continues – motivation is continually stimulated. Play can be seen to be flowing when a child or children are fully absorbed.

The play process

So the whole play process can be seen as an inner and potentially compelling drive, which sets up a cycle of playing that eventually breaks down over a period of time.

Here are some examples of differing play cycles within their frames, which *may* indicate the need for some change to the play environment or other intervention (see Intervention Modes and Play Environments in Chapter 5).

Key question

Each of the figures is indicating that a playworker needs to respond in some way. How would you respond to the needs expressed by Figures 3.5, 3.6 and 3.7?

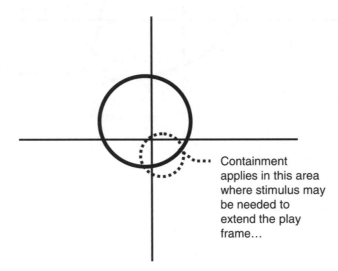

Containment applies in this area where stimulus may be needed to extend the play frame…

Figure 3.5 Containment 1.

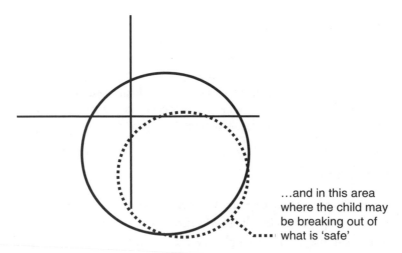

…and in this area where the child may be breaking out of what is 'safe'

Figure 3.6 Containment 2.

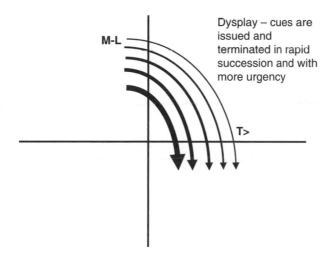

M-L

Dysplay – cues are issued and terminated in rapid succession and with more urgency

T>

Figure 3.7 Dysplay.
Source: Taken from 'The 'The Playground as therapeutic space: playwork as healing'. Else and Sturrock (1998)

Play types

Because of its enigmatic nature, and therefore in some way to better try to capture it, play is sometimes broken down or categorized, into various different types. Here are some examples of this:

1 Social play – Solitary; looking on; joining in; simple co-operative; complex co-operative
2 SPICE – Social; physical; intellectual; creative; emotional play
3 Games – High verbal content; high imaginative content; high physical content
4 Experienced play; intuitive play; pretended play; expressive play; cognitive play; physical play (1994:57), Wada's Classification
5 Free play (play opportunity); structured play (play activity)
6 Mind or subjective play; solitary play; playful behaviours; informal social play; vicarious audience play; performance play; celebrations and festivals; contests (games and sport); risky or deep play Sutton-Smith (1997:4–5)
7 Progress, imagination, selfhood, power, identity and fate and chaos.

Hughes in his *Taxonomy of Play Types* (2002a) identified sixteen different types of play as follows. These have been widely accepted by the playwork world and form part of the current National Standards for Playwork. We have built on his descriptions and examples in the following list.

Symbolic play

Play which allows control, gradual exploration and increased understanding without being out of one's depth, by using symbols, that is, objects, designs or signs to represent people, ideas or qualities. For example, using a piece of wood to symbolize a person or a weapon; a piece of string to symbolize a wedding ring; a length of rope to symbolize a boundary; a carrot to symbolize a microphone; building a shrine or creating a flag.

Exploratory play

'Finding-out' – play that accesses factual information about an environment and engages with the area or thing and, either by manipulation or movement, assesses its properties, possibilities and content. For example stacking bricks, taking a camera apart, digging 'to Australia'.

Object play

'Problem-solving' – play which uses infinite and interesting sequences of hand-eye manipulations and movements. For example, examination and novel use of any object, for example, cloth, rope, bubble wrap, paintbrush, cup. The fascination here is with the object itself and what it can do or be (regardless of what its 'proper use' might be).

Rough and tumble play

Close encounter play which is less to do with fighting and more to do with touching, tickling, gauging relative strength, discovering physical flexibility and the exhilaration of display. Finding out and testing one's own and other's limits; learning social and interpersonal codes of physical conduct. For example, playful fighting, wrestling and chasing where the children are obviously unhurt and giving every indication that they are enjoying themselves.

Socio-dramatic play

The enactment of real and potential experiences of an intense personal, social, domestic or interpersonal nature, that is, the child re-creates scenes from his own life. For example, playing at house, going to the shops, being mums and dads, organizing a meal, having a row, holding a funeral, going to the divorce courts etc. The child also sometimes acts out emotions too scary to express in real life – this can be therapeutic.

Dramatic play

Play which dramatizes events in which the child is not a direct participator, that is, re-creating scenes from others' lives or from the television or theatre, for example, presentation of a TV show; an event on the street or in the news; a religious or festive event; a birth or death; or being famous footballers or a band in a recent match or concert – often done for an audience.

Social play

Play during which the rules and criteria for social engagement, interaction and communication can be revealed, explored and amended. Any social or interactive situation which contains an expectation on all parties that they will discuss and abide by certain rules, customs or protocols, for example, games, conversations, making something together, challenging, discussing . . .

Communication play

Play using words, nuances or gestures, for example, mime, jokes, play acting, 'mickey' taking, singing, debate, poetry, graffiti, swearing, making up languages/words/slang, storytelling. Creating a reaction and exploring the impact.

Creative play (inventive play)

Play which allows a new response, an expression of self; the transformation of information; awareness of new connections and new insights, with an element of surprise. It is about focused but spontaneous creation with a wide range of materials and tools for its own sake,

Photo 3.1 Rock star today?

with real freedom and not necessarily an end result. It could be small or large scale, individual or group.

Deep play

Play that develops survival skills and conquers fear, through the child encountering what they perceive to be high-risk physical and emotional experiences, for example, leaping onto an aerial runway, giving an alternative opinion that is likely to be rejected, balancing on a high beam. The risk will be from the child's perspective (certainly not the adults') and so the same experience could be deep play for one child and not the next.

Fantasy play

Play which rearranges the world in the child's way – a way which is complete fantasy and unreal, for example, being superheroes, aliens, goblins, timelords, flying a UFO, casting spells, saving the world from certain destruction . . .

Imaginative play

Play where the conventional rules that govern the physical world do not apply, but is still based on reality. For example, imagining you are, or pretending to be, a tree, a ship or an animal, patting a dog which isn't there, having an invisible friend, imagining a table is a bus or a cave . . .

Role play

Play exploring identity and ways of being and doing, although not normally of an intense personal, social, domestic or interpersonal nature. Often imitating someone or trying out something seen but not experienced e.g. driving a car, playing dead, being a clown or a shopkeeper.

Locomotor play

Movement in any and every direction – up down, along, at various speeds and seemingly for its own sake. For example, chase, tag, hide and seek, tree climbing, rolling, jumping, dancing: Experiencing the possibilities of one's body within a particular environment – includes ranging.

Mastery play

Generally expressed by taking (and feeling) control of the physical and affective ingredients of the natural environment; for example, digging holes and tunnels in earth or sand; changing the course of streams; gaining a new skill, for example, a jump across a river, or riding a bike . . .

Recapitulative play

Play that displays aspects of human evolutionary history, stored and passed on through our genes and manifested when children play spontaneously – often stimulated by aspects of the outdoor environment like forests and shallow pools/rivers. For example lighting fires, engaging in spontaneous rituals and songs, dressing up in historic clothes/uniforms and role-playing, playing wars and making weapons, growing and cooking things, creating ancient style communities, building shelters, creating languages and religions.

Key question

What play type(s) might be occurring here?

Photo 3.2 Swimming on grass!

In some settings playworkers have tried to plan play activities slavishly around the notion of development through certain types of play for example, a construction table has been provided with the assumption that exploratory play will take place at it and the children will develop numeracy, spatial awareness and fine motor skills.

In reality if we allow children to play freely and flexibly they may well use the construction materials in a way an adult would not anticipate and if there are any developmental benefits they may not be the ones that were anticipated for example, a child may combine construction material with sand and water in a hole in the ground to make a brew to cast spells with. Which play types are reflected in that scenario and what if any developmental benefits could there be?

Reflection – Jacky

I remember a play session that I facilitated during a community centre open day one Halloween. I took in some props/loose parts – dressing up clothes, old sheets, masks, a cauldron and big wooden spoon, lots of jars and tubs of things that looked potentially fascinating or disgusting such as capers, prunes, coloured pasta, liquorice strings, slime, twigs, plastic frogs, spiders, beetles, glitter, stars, tinsel, etc. etc. The children and I told some spooky stories and they spontaneously started dressing up and making potions in the cauldron using not only the things that I had made available but also going outside and collecting other stuff and chucking in all sorts of unlikely found and natural materials! It started with mainly younger children but then a whole load of slightly bored older children came in, first of all to sneer but then they got into playing and cast some brilliant spells and made up wonderful chants and weird dances around the cauldron. They also made up a Halloween rap song and the whole thing grew a life of its own as play events often seem to. On reflection there were many play types that manifested themselves including – symbolic, object, social, communication, creative, deep, fantasy, imaginative, role-play, locomotor and recapitulative play. I could not have planned for this. Interestingly, but unbeknown to me at the time, Marc Armitage (2001:53) reports on repeated evidence, from play audits, of particular features, in school playgrounds, that act as 'cues' for a type of fantasy 'pretend' play that involves witches or other monsters making spells in cauldrons or 'stewpots'.

Classifying play into types can certainly help with observation of children playing and planning an environment for play to ensure that it offers the potential for the realization of all play types. However being prescriptive may cause its own problems. There may for instance be other play types as yet not classified – a number have been postulated recently such as nurture play, sexual play and sadistic play. Would we adults necessarily want to plan for all of these? I think not! There may perhaps be play types based around emotions and feelings such as 'anger play' or 'embarrassment play'. Elsewhere we have imagined three-dimensional play types that have thinking; feeling and doing facets to them and an over-arching 'interaction' play type that could contain all others and yet not be a constraint to play.

Play behaviour

Can play behaviour be identified and classified in the same way as play types, or are they one and the same thing? In *The First Claim* (2001) Hughes has suggested that there should be a diversity of play narratives and activity types and that play experiences should bring children into contact with nature, ecosystems and loose parts in order for play to manifest itself. He further suggests that within the right setting if the behaviour is freely chosen, personally directed, and intrinsically motivated, in a secure context, spontaneous, goalless and under the child's control it will be play. But how can we mere playworkers determine all of this?

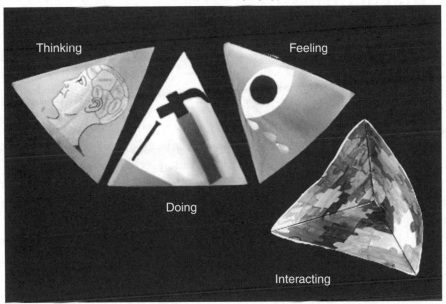

Figure 3.8 Playing with fire.

How do you know when a child is playing? Is it what they do, why they are doing what they are doing, when they do it or can it only be a person who is playing who knows whether they are playing or not? Can it be play if you cannot be seen to be doing anything? How do you know if a child is working out a homework problem in their head or daydreaming about riding a turquoise unicorn above the clouds? Does a baby recognize when it starts to play that this is behaviour that is different to say feeding or is feeding, play for a baby because it is freely chosen, personally directed and intrinsically motivated as well as being enjoyable?

We adults may think we know what play is and therefore know when a child is playing, because we have experienced that which we call play and because we have developed to believe that we can determine that which is real and not real. Children and the more spiritual of adults can easily mix the two together to form a different type of reality, one that exists in reality but is not real and therefore may not be able to be seen. We therefore may not be able to determine play behaviour by observation alone. (See more on observation in Chapter 5.) If the play cycle within a play frame is used as the model within which to locate play behaviour (which may or may not fit into a particular play type) it gives the playworker a context within which he or she can call upon his or her knowledge of play types and repertoire of interventions to select the most appropriate intervention mode for that particular situation.

In order to broaden our notions about play, in all its manifestations, a dedicated few within the playwork world continue to delve into the complexity which is play and give us other ways of thinking about it. Play Mechanisms are one such response to this delving. They provide us with another tool for analysing what is going on when children play.

Play mechanisms

A mechanism is the way something works or is brought about. Play Mechanisms then are a way of describing the relationship between the child and his or her play environment – It's not 'what the child is doing' but 'the way that the child is doing it'. Twelve mechanisms have been identified in *The First Claim – Desirable processes* (2002) and they are based on an interpretation of theoretical data and from playwork experience.

The mechanisms enable us to move beyond just identifying what types of play children are engaging in, but also to consider the way in which the children are involved in playing. For instance a child might be playing socio-dramatic play, perhaps playing out a scary visit to an accident and emergency department at a hospital when he had fallen out of a tree and been concussed, but while playing be totally immersed in the play so that it's more real than that which is actually going on around him. The child is 'zoned out' from the real world. On another occasion the same child might be engaged in the same play type with the same general theme but perhaps be involved in calibration by demonstrating what might have happened had he fallen from a different angle, height etc. A child may be involved in locomotor play while also ranging through the play environment equally she could be involved in fantasy play pretending to be a super-hero ranging through a city.

Here is a brief overview of the twelve mechanisms.

Reflection opportunity

Observe a child or children playing and try to match your observational evidence to one or other of the mechanisms below. Can you interpret which play mechanism is operating? From your own interpretation of what you have read about play and from your own experience and reflection can you think of other ways that you might describe a child's involvement? Would your description fit within the principles of playwork? How can you use your knowledge of play mechanisms to improve your work with children?

Reflection opportunity

Can you think of examples of children playing that fit each one?

Figure 3.9 Play mechanisms.

Play mechanism	Definition
Immersion	Being engaged in a play experience with such focus and intensity, that temporary sensory dissociation from external reality occurs
Non-specialization	Being and feeling so competent with a continually changing and diverse range of play choices, that no individual play type or group of play types is allowed to dominate behaviour
Bio-identification	Frequently interacting with a diverse range of natural elements, non-humans and other flora and fauna in preference to playing within narrow social or cultural parameters
Combinatorial flexibility	Freely associating with the play space in ways which enable the use of novel combinations of behaviour and which develop an evolving combinatorial repertoire
Neophilia	Showing a frequent attraction to new and novel environmental features and characteristics
Repetition	Repeating particular basic actions or patterns of behaviour, while gradually incorporating minor and major variations to them
Absorption	Integration of externally generated stimuli in the form of behaviour, language, culture and values into one's own identity without being taught or instructed
Co-ordination	Moving different parts of the body, in relation to eye and object in a balanced, efficient and fluid manner
Abstraction	Visualizing and rearranging or restructuring objects and ideas in and into their component parts
Ranging	Moving through, exploring and engaging with an ever-widening area of the play environment
Recapitulation	Engaging in 'evolutionary or recapitulative play' some of which will be more reminiscent of tribal, hunter-gatherer and pre-tribal behaviours
Calibration	Developing a relative relationship with the world based upon physical comparison – weight, height, width and speed of movement – by playfully interacting with an ever-changing physical environment

Source: Taken from *First Claim – Desirable Processes* (2002)

Play and risk taking

The way that playworkers think and behave about risk is one of the things that make playwork a distinct style of interaction with children. (2008:68)

It is during play that children take their initial risks in life, for example, a toddler climbing onto a table or a child hanging upside down on the branch of a tree and risking injury or death; children 'performing' in front of others and risking ridicule. Gladwin (2008:69) says that 'play is one of the arenas where the dominant paradigm of risk avoidance sometimes gives way to an alternative paradigm of voluntary risk taking'. Gordon (2002:6) suggests that there is a sliding-scale spectrum of risk taking across all children that extends from a child

Playing with fire

Photo 3.3 Two girls at beach fire.

who exhibits no risk taking in play to a child that exhibits a high degree of risk-taking behaviour including Deep Play. She suggests that there are biological, genetic, evolutionary and social reasons as to why this risk or sensation-seeking behaviour is manifested during play, but of the fact that it is important, she and we have no doubt.

Tim Gill, in *No Fear Growing Up* (2007) points out that it is easier to collect quantitative information about the negative side of risk taking because there are many statistics to tell how many children have, for instance, been injured in settings. Most information about the benefits of play is qualitative. For instance Tim (2007:42) speaks of the anxieties of some adults related to allowing children to play fight or engage in gun play as they may be blamed if the children get hurt or other adults may find it unacceptable. He suggests however that if children (boys particularly) are deprived of these experiences they may well be less able to keep themselves safe as they grow up as these experiences help them to negotiate tricky social situations. Psychologists believe that children learn to read the communication of their opponents during play fighting and learn to understand when something is play or genuinely threatening.

Because of the belief in children's natural desire and need to take risk, playworkers must manage risk in a way that balances benefits with risks. Where benefits seem to outweigh risks, measures can be put in place to enable the play to happen. Gladwin (2008:71) says there is a paradox where 'nobody wants a child to be injured, yet a playground where, no accidents ever happen is unlikely to be meeting children's play needs'. This is difficult for many adults, particularly those who have lost contact with their own childhood play, forgetting the risks that they themselves took.

There are many unproven, yet deeply held and widely recognized beliefs about the potential key benefits of risk taking, during play, for children such as: self-confidence; self-awareness; capacity to assess risk and therefore develop survival skills; the development of skills associated with the particular risky behaviour, for example, bike riding, swimming, singing; problem solving and divergent thinking; adaptation skills; life experiences gained (many of us can remember 'surviving' various escapades and these stories become part of our life history); social status etc. Gordon (1999) further suggests that if opportunities for risk taking in play, are not made available to children, those of them who are natural risk takers, will often create their own opportunities which may be both more dangerous and also outside the law. We would go further and suggest that if opportunities for risk taking in play are not made available for all children, regardless of their natural tendencies children may well not develop the capacity to assess risk for themselves and to become independent. The inability to self-assess risk means that a child is constantly beholden to others and also potentially unable to recognize that which is dangerous. Hughes (2001a) even thinks that children need to confront their own immortality and cosmic insignificance by experiencing risk to find their place in the world.

Gill suggests (2007:61) that there has been a 'collective failure of nerve about children's need to learn for themselves how to cope with many types of risks. The regulatory services such as the Health and Safety Executive and Ofsted have grown so much in size and reach, that the prescribed procedural approach that they develop and use can limit the scope for flexibility and professional judgement'. Playworkers have a duty to children and society to find ways to continue researching and influencing views on children's risk taking in play and ways to safely manage this essential need for risky opportunities in children's play provision.

This topic links to the following section on play deprivation but will also be further discussed and developed in Chapter 6 in the section on Health and Safety where risk assessment procedures will be outlined.

Reflection – Jacky

I remember on a trip to the seaside a little group of us children found a huge old inflated inner tube that we took into the sea and played on. We played on it in the shallow waters to begin with, sitting on it, lying on it, jumping on and off it, paddling along on it, hanging on to it etc. and gradually taking it further and further out into deeper waters while swirling around in the increasingly rough waves of the North Sea. Our parents had told us to bring it in but I had to have 'just one more go' and got thrown up onto the shingles and then sucked back into the water and out of the inner tube and I was tumbled around in the undertow. I was terrified that I would drown, but once I partly staggered and was partly pulled to safety, it became a great tale of 'daring do'. Obviously this could have had a tragic outcome but our memories are part of who we become.

> ### Reflection opportunity
>
> Reflect on your own risky play as a child. What benefits do you think you gained from them?

Play deprivation

If we believe in any of the theories and concepts related to play then we must also believe that play is one of the vitally important processes of a child's life. If a child is unable or prevented from playing freely and flexibly in a rich play environment then we must also believe that they can suffer from play deprivation. The playwork world suggests that the consequences of children suffering play deprivation 'are potentially damaging to the healthy development of those children' (2003:59) and indeed to the well-being of our future societies. We feel we are seeing some of these effects already with the rise in antisocial behaviour and lack of sense of community so often portrayed in our young people. The playwork approach to providing for play through the creation of rich play environments, reflective practice and appropriate interventions (see Chapter 5) then can be seen as both preventative and curative, part of the antidote for children who are suffering play deprivation.

Ali illustrates this with a close-to-home example.

Reflection – Ali

A child I have known well had cancer and from the ages of 5–7 had a triple Hickman line in his chest which meant he could not go swimming or do any body contact sport or rough and tumble play. He keenly felt the loss of all this and almost as soon as he had the line removed and was able to be 'normal' (his words) he was getting himself into trouble for what was labelled both aggressive and 'tell-tale' behaviour. Actually all he was doing was joining in with play fighting etc., but he had not had the experience over time (as the others had had) to be able to judge what he was physically capable of. Consequently he was too rough and hurtful to others and wincing and crying when he got shoved back. He is 13 now and told me recently that he still considers himself behind his peers – he is much more cautious about what his mates deem everyday behaviour. Certainly I see him taking fewer risks than others his age, but from my perspective, the 'damage' is more social. The loss of rough and tumble play for over two years at such an important time has had long-lasting effects on his peer relationships – he finds it really hard to socially 'joust' and has real difficulty with everyday banter and teasing.

In this chapter we have examined some of the widely accepted concepts that inform playwork practice at this time. We have looked at a framework for play; the whole process of playing; that which constitutes play behaviour; the links between play and risk taking and the dangers of play deprivation. As time advances thinking on these complex notions will also advance and help us to better understand what is going on when children play and therefore how better to respond to them. In order to understand children's play it is important to think about children. Chapter 4 does just that.

Further reading

Brown, F. and Taylor, C. (Eds) (2008) *Foundations of Playwork*. Maidenhead: Open University Press McGraw-Hill Education.

Hughes, B. (2001) *The First Claim . . . A Framework for Playwork Quality Assessment*, Cardiff: Play Wales.

Hughes, B. (2002) *The First Claim – Desirable Processes. A Framework for Advanced Quality Assessment*. Cardiff: Play Wales.

Hughes, B. (2002a) *A Playworkers Taxonomy of Play Types, 2nd edition*. London: PlayLink.

Play Wales (2005) *Playwork Principles*. Cardiff: Play Wales.

Sturrock, G. (2003) *The Ludic Third*. The British Institute of Therapeutic Playwork. Sheffield: Ludemos.

Sturrock, G. Russell, W. and Else, P. (2004) *Towards Ludogogy Parts 1, 11 and 111. The Art of Being and Becoming through Play: The Birmingham Paper*. Sheffield: Ludemos Associates.

References

Armitage, M. (2001) 'The Ins and Outs of School Playground Play: Children's Use of "play places"' in Bishop, C. and Curtis, M. (Eds) *Play Today in the Primary School Playground*. Buckingham: Open University Press.

Brown, F. (2003) 'Compound Flexibility: The Role of Playwork in Child Development' in Brown, F. (Ed.) *Playwork Theory and Practice*. Buckingham: Open University Press.

Else, P. and Sturrock, G. (1998) *The Playground as Therapeutic Space: Playwork as Healing*. A paper for Play in a Changing Society: Research, Design, Application. The IPA/USA Triennial National Conference, June 1998.

Gladwin, M. (2008) 'The Concept of Risk in Play and Playwork' in Brown, F. and Taylor, C. (Eds) *Foundations of Playwork*. Maidenhead: Open University Press McGraw Hill Education.

Gordon (1999) 'Riskogenics Part 1, an Exploration of Risk Taking in Children's Play' in Hughes, B. (1999) *Play Ed Conference Proceedings*. Ely. Play Education.

Gordon, C. (2002) *Riskogenics Part 2*. Ely: Playtonics.

Hughes, B. (2001) *The First Claim . . . A Framework for Playwork Quality Assessment*. Cardiff: Play Wales.

Hughes, B. (2001a) *Evolutionary Playwork and Reflective Analytic Practice*. London: Routledge.

Hughes, B. (2002) *The First Claim – Desirable Processes. A Framework for Advanced Quality Assessment*. Cardiff: Play Wales.

Hughes, B. (2002a) *A Playworkers Taxonomy of Play Types, 2nd edition*. London: PlayLink.

Ibid.

Kilvington, J. (2007) Performance notes. Unpublished.

Play Wales (2005) *Playwork Principles*. Cardiff: Play Wales.

SkillsActive (2005) *National Occupational Standards for Playwork Level 3*. London: SkillsActive.

SkillsActive (2006) *Quality Training, Quality Play 2006–2011*. London: SkillsActive.

Sturrock, G. Russell, W. and Else, P. (2004) *Towards Ludogogy Parts 1, 11 and 111. The Art of Being and Becoming through Play: The Birmingham Paper*. Sheffield: Ludemos Associates.

Sutton-Smith, B. (1997) *The Ambiguity of Play*. U.S.A.: Harvard University Press.

Takeuchi, M. (1994) 'Children's Play in Japan' in Roopnarine, J. L. Johnson, J. E. and Hooper, F. H. (Eds) *Children's Play in Diverse Cultures*. Albany: State University of New York Press .

4 The Child

The title of this chapter is in itself a misnomer, because there is no such being as 'the child'. Many of us would readily agree that every child is an individual with their own needs and interests. But, as with many things, there is a difference between 'espoused theory' and 'theory in practice' (Argyris & Schon, 1974:6–7), or to put it more crudely there is a contrast between what we say and what we do. This distinction is usually not intentional because we often do not recognize it exists. We 'see through a glass darkly' (Corinthians) because to be truly objective about who children are, requires us to sit outside our experiences, our culture, our society and our time. This chapter takes us on a more historical journey to see where our current understanding about children has come from and how this view of the child affects our playwork.

What is a child

What is a child? How do they differ from adults? Are the differences purely physiological? What is an adult? How does a child become an adult and when? Can we be sure of any of our answers to these questions?

Reflection opportunity

We will all have been influenced in many ways to perceive children in the ways that we each do. How do you 'see' children? Which of the following statements do you find yourself agreeing or disagreeing with?

Children will be wild if they do not have firm boundaries
Children should always be listened to
Children are adults in the making
Children learn how to behave from adults
Children learn how to behave from children
Children don't know what's good for them
Children can keep themselves safe
Children need to learn respect
Children are thoughtful, responsible, capable people
Children have their own culture, peculiar to themselves

Of course in reality, none of these and other such statements can be either true or false, but our answers to them can sometimes show the trends and influences in our own attitudes towards children and if we work or live with children, then we should make efforts to recognize and question these patterns and pressures. Who are children really? What are their needs and capabilities? What is a 'good' childhood?

Are children blank pages – unformed people 'who through literacy, education, reason, self-control and shame may be made into a civilised adult'? (Postman, 1994:59). Or are children innocents, important in their own right and born with 'capacities for candour, curiosity and spontaneity' (Postman, 1994:59) with 'access to levels of understanding greater than those available for adults'? (Cunningham, 2006:134).

These two opposing views about children's nature that embody the Protestant and Romantic movements in the eighteenth century still have influence and are still largely unresolved today.

Our view of children cannot help but be coloured by past and current societal attitudes and these too, have changed and are changing rapidly. The lives of children a hundred years ago, fifty years ago and even twenty years ago were very different and many of these differences are not necessarily due to external situations or conditions but to the ways they were perceived and therefore treated by adults.

This is still the case the world over – the prevailing needs and beliefs of adults in each society will dictate the ways in which children lead their lives. Children can hold great responsibility or none, can look after themselves or be looked after, can have much freedom or very little, can question and help shape social policy or be its recipients, can wage war or be its victims . . . It does seem to us that in Britain at least, the most prevalent attitude towards children is a patronizing one – however 'positively' or 'negatively' this might be expressed – adults 'know best'. But do they? Just because we were children once, does that equip us to

Photo 4.1 Leaves glorious leaves.

understand children and childhood? Just because we are adults now, does that entitle us to define and decide who children are and what they shall or shall not do?

Reflection opportunity

Stop and think for a moment about what you personally think about children and who they are and how they should be treated. Where did your views come from? Your childhood experiences? Your parents? Your work experiences as an adult? Books? The media? Children you see around you today?

A history of childhood

Much has been written in the last few decades about children both in the present and in the past. Volumes on the history and social constructions of childhood and child development theories – many of them conflicting – now abound and it is not the purpose of this chapter to specifically explore or champion any of these, but to draw attention to some of the concepts therein. It is worth bearing in mind however, that it is adults who have written the majority of these tomes about children; children themselves have little or no contribution.

The very idea of childhood as a specific and separate time to adulthood is a moving feast and indeed the concept of adolescence as another distinct phase is fairly recent and a subject of regular debate. Philippe Aries was an influential historian in the 1960s with his 'Centuries of Childhood', in which he argues that childhood had been invented in Europe in the fifteenth–eighteenth centuries. Prior to this, children – once they could walk and talk – seemed to have been regarded as miniature adults and they were therefore not shielded or removed from any of the realities of life, harsh or otherwise. During these centuries however, Aries states that attitudes slowly changed and children began to be seen as different to adults, with specific needs for care, protection and education.

This idea of the invention of childhood inspired others and Lloyd de Mause's *The History of Childhood* and then Lawrence Stone's *The Family, Sex and Marriage in England 1500–1800* took up the theme, examining parochial, biographical and educational texts and records and even artwork for evidence of the everyday lives and attitudes of adults and children. Neil Postman further contributed by arguing that the concept of childhood as a different state to adulthood was a direct result of the birth of literacy because:

a the communication of ideas was no longer solely oral and therefore could be more widespread;

b society became divided into the literate and the illiterate;

c places of learning were created for those who wanted to become literate; and

d these places eventually became schools – for children.

In the medieval world he says,

> There had been no need for the idea of childhood for everyone shared the same information environment and therefore lived in the same social and intellectual world. But as the printing press played out its hand, it became obvious that a new kind of *adulthood* had been invented. From print onward the young would have to *become* adults and they would have to do it by learning to read, by entering the world of typography. And in order to accomplish that they would require education. Therefore European civilisation reinvented schools and by so doing it made childhood a necessity. (Postman, 1994:36)

The detail contained in all these volumes is impressive and the case often well put, but Aries, de Mause and Stone also all argue from a 'progressive' perspective, that is, they feel that adult treatment of children has vastly improved with time.

Linda Pollock has been critical of this approach and in her *Forgotten Children: Parent-child Relations 1500–1900* she claims that the evidence put forward can be interpreted very differently when put into the social and religious contexts of the time; for example many diaries and letters feature only middle class and/or male perspectives, who therefore write with a particular emphasis. Her view is that as now, most parents cared for their children and did their best for them and she cites numerous examples of this throughout history.

Perhaps then what has changed for European children in the last few hundred years is not so much a growth in parental care but a slow recognition in wider society that children are a group in society that have certain needs. Over time this has evolved in legislation to ensure these diverse needs are addressed and more recently there has been acceptance of children having legal rights and entitlements, embodied in the United Nations Convention on the Rights of the Child (UNCRC). This of course has happened and continues to happen for other groups in society – women, disabled people and ethnic minority groups and so on. Perhaps the mark of a 'civilised' society is not the way that individual parents care for their children, but the way society itself regards and treats them.

As Thomas (1998–2009) says

> As there is little evidence of what childhood was really like in the past, it is incredibly difficult for historians to reconstruct the life of a child, much more the 'experience' of being a child. In so many ways, the history of childhood is a history that slips through our fingers. Few parents have left written records of how they reared their children and the number of children who have left us their story is fewer still. It is largely because of this lack of evidence and because the evidence that does remain – advice literature, journals and letters, are so open to differing interpretations, that historians have divided over major issues such as whether children were loved and wanted in the past, the way parents viewed their children, and the treatment they received.

Cunningham's book *The Invention of Childhood* which was serialized on Radio 4 this year, covers a thousand years of childhood and does feature children's own stories and comments where these have been found, in a heart-warming attempt to give children of the past their own voice. A few other historians have also tried to right the balance in the last couple of decades and have been determined to focus on children's own actions and narratives (see for example Hanawalt, 1993 and Nasaw, 1986).

Whatever the truth about adults feelings and attitudes towards children, there is no doubt however, that over time children were slowly separated from adults and no longer allowed the same access to the 'adult' world with its values, appetites and secrets. Postman contends that this gave rise to a 'well-developed idea of shame' (1994:9) a 'not in front of the children' ethic that became ingrained in adults and has perhaps given us the 'adults-know-best' perspective so widespread today.

Of course the ability to read and the availability of books also meant that ideas about the needs and nature of children – and how best to rear them – began to be written and by the end of the eighteenth century there was much printed instruction and advice. This still goes on today of course – ideas on what is and is not good for children have their day and can sometimes influence whole generations before the next 'new' ideas emerge. Just within the last fifty years, from Truby King (1934) to Benjamin Spock (1945) to Jean Liedloff (1975) to Penelope Leach (1989), parents have been cajoled to bottle feed then breast feed, to physically punish children and then to reason with them, to make them eat their greens and then to give them choice, to give them freedom to roam and then to rein them in and protect them . . .

'Childhood may be a biological fact (but) the way in which it is understood and lived is socially determined, within an actively negotiated set of social relations' (Moss and Petrie, 2002:20).

Key questions

What are the current ideas in society on rearing children and what is their impact? Which ones do you agree with and why? Which ones do you not agree with and why? Where do these ideas come from?

Just as there have been diverse views on children's historical lives, there have been proposed many theories on children's development and subsequent debates on the research methodologies behind these.

These theories have been categorized in a number of ways; the most simple being 'nature' and 'nurture'; that is, children develop according to their preordained genetic code, or, their development is shaped by what and who is around them and their own consequent passive or active reactions and responses. The nature-nurture debate has raged for decades, although it is now generally accepted – even on both sides – that both are true.

Within the 'nature school' are the maturationists; those who believe that development has a biological basis and is a naturally occurring process in healthy children. Beginning with Arnold Gesell (1943), the maturationists gave us the 'ages and stages' perspective; the developmental milestones that all children should achieve and were very influential in the 1950s. This is now viewed more flexibly as we have recognized that these norms can vary widely according to individual interest and cultural practices. 'It is possible to build up a flexible use of developmental norms without signing up to rigid maturational theory' (Lindon, 2007:20).

Also residing mostly within the 'nature school' are the biologists and zoologists that have made connections between animal and human development. These led to:

Child development theories

a Attachment Theory (Bowlby, 1969) – the concept that without a strong and instinctive emotional bond with another (usually mother, but it is now understood that this is not exclusively the case), mammals will fail to thrive.

b Practice Theory (Groos, 1901, Young, 1978) – this suggests that instincts and behaviour patterns essential for survival have to be practised in early life and that this naturally occurs through playing.

c Recapitulation Theory (Hall, 1904, Reaney, 1916, Wilber, 1996) – the idea that children naturally 'play out' the previous stages of human history as they grow up, for example, animal, savage, nomad, pastoral and tribal, in order to adapt to the present and continue to evolve as a species. Hughes (2001) has recently built on this to propose that the breadth of recapitulative play is essential for all aspects of human health and that deprivation of this will have serious evolutionary consequences.

d Neuroscience – recent and ongoing research in this fascinating area looks into how the brain grows and works and affects behaviour and development. Brain growth occurs through stimulating millions of neural connections which in turn help to make patterns of meaning – these patterns are continually checked, changed and renewed as new information, insights and connections are added. The brain is designed to solve problems and keep us alert, alive and able. Play is highly significant in promoting brain growth because its free and random nature stimulates more neural connections and more checking of neural pathways (see Burghardt, 2005).

On the nurture side of the fence, there are theorists who believe that a child's environment influences their learning and behaviour – the environmentalists who think that children are passive recipients of experience and the constructivists who think that children actively respond to and create new experiences. These can all be loosely divided into three theory types.

Learning theory

a Behaviourism – the behaviourists such as Watson (1970) and Skinner (1953), stated that humans develop by learning through experiences and that such experiences can therefore be controlled in order to produce or 'condition' the desired growth or learning. Conditioning operates by causing and reinforcing certain responses by linking them to specific stimuli and/or rewards. Bandura (1977) took this further to add the process of 'modelling' – children will closely observe the behaviour and expressions of others (children and adults) and then copy these, including the underlying beliefs and ideas that these may embody.

b Cognitive development – Piaget (1969) proposed that children actively construct their own understanding in different ways at different ages, but individually exploring and experiencing what is around them. The details of his stages are now mostly disputed, but his ideas were radical at the time and generated a lot of further research. Vygotsky (1994) was very interested in how children both teach and learn through social interaction with each other and also with adults – what he called the zone of proximal development. Bruner (1986) developed this perspective to help adults be observant and sensitive to children's interests and therefore provide materials for them to explore and return to and also to spark new ideas or ways of using them.

Reflection opportunity

Children do not play in order to learn, but they certainly learn through play and seek out stimulation through their playing. They will examine and investigate the world around them through using all their senses, their minds and their bodies. They will imitate others and try out all kinds of roles and explore different values in order to comprehend their meaning and significance. Can you think of play you have seen that fits here?

Psychoanalytic theory

Theories under this heading are many and diverse but the basic tenet is that behaviour (and therefore development) is influenced by our feelings and thoughts, many of which are unconscious and due to previous and sometimes traumatic experiences. Such experiences, especially in early childhood, when children are too young to make full sense of them and may therefore negatively interpret or respond to them, can lead to defence mechanisms, suppression, anxiety, aggression and inferiority, if not understood, treated or resolved through play.

Freud (1914) was the main instigator of psychoanalytic tradition, although his approach has significantly diversified. Erikson (1950) introduced the concept of psychosocial developmental stages where children have to find the balance between opposing dilemmas at different ages; for example, 'is this person trustworthy or not?', 'shall I do what I want or what someone else wants?'

Reflection opportunity

Children themselves work hard at making sense of their experiences and play is their natural medium for doing so. They 'play out' things that frighten and confuse them (this is why so many play narratives are violent and regularly have battles between goodies and baddies). They will also use fantasy play to make reality more manageable and feel more in control of themselves and events around them – again their play content often features aliens, monsters, fairies and superheroes. Can you think of examples of play you have seen and/or heard recently that show this?

Sociocultural theory

This approach has evolved over the last few decades, arguing that children cannot develop apart from the groups and systems they belong to – how they each physically, emotionally, socially, intellectually and spiritually develop is all affected by family culture, educational ethos, friendship dynamics, community relations, religious expectations and current political strategies and so on. Bronfenbrenner (1979) presented a model of concentric circles to illustrate the complexity of individual human development within an ever-changing society within an evolving world.

Reflection opportunity

Children's social play is intriguing and complex. They develop cues, codes and rules and secret societies that keep experimenting with concepts of ownership, membership, democracy and justice. They particularly love to test out the power of adults while still externally conforming to adult rules and come up with highly organized small 'rebellions' that achieve this without overt violation. Can you describe examples?

How children are perceived

How does all this affect how we personally relate to and perceive children? All these different theories have their place in a wider understanding of how children develop. A holistic approach recognizes that human development is not linear but probably more like a spider's web where many diverse experiences all reverberate across and connect to those that have gone before. Moss and Petrie however, say that 'particular disciplines, professions, agencies, settings and policy areas each create or construct particular versions of childhood and images of the child shaped by their own theories, understandings and perspectives' (2002:20). In other words, adults in different organizations see children through organizational glasses as a particular kind of child.

So rather than see lots of individual unique human beings, we see certain sorts-of-children. For example, in Early Years we see 'the toddler', 'the preschooler' (which in itself seems to describe an unfulfilled stage that will only gain status with school attendance), the 'child-with-working-parents'. In Social Services we hear about 'the newly-arrived child', 'the looked-after child' and 'the abused child'. In Health Trusts we talk about 'the hyperactive child' and 'the disabled child'. In Education we discuss 'children with learning difficulties' and 'children with behavioural problems' and 'children from lone-parent or step-families'.

These are all labels that confine and stereotype individual children, yet conversations and comments like 'He's fostered so he'll have all kinds of issues then . . .' and 'She's got Asperger's

Photo 4.2 Who am I today?

syndrome – have we got enough staff to cope?' occur every day across the children's work-force without us batting an eyelid. We think we know a child because we've met their family, know where they live, what language they speak or what religion they have. But these are all social constructs that can stop us seeing the individual whole child before us. Children are being viewed through the lens of the service providing for them, which can never give the whole picture.

Do we also have a certain sort-of-child in playwork? Is our image of 'the freely playing child' any more or less accurate? Is it true that all children are naturally adventurous – cut up worms/love rain? Could we be just expressing 'the nostalgic and idealised view the middle-class and the middle-aged have of their own apparently tranquil post-war upbringing' (Brockliss and Rousseau, 2003:4)? Playworkers who are truly reflective will recognize they cannot be immune from both external and internal influences and strive to develop a greater awareness of these in their own thinking and practice. We have to be prepared to learn from children and from our feelings – we may discover that some of our deeply held 'musts' are clearly not right for our children (and probably never were for us either).

While all of us who work with children may be subject to or influenced by particular con-structs, there does also seem to currently be two over-riding societal views in Britain about children. The first is that they are 'weak, poor and needy' (Moss and Petrie, 2002:55). This is not to say that there are not people and organizations who question this and who lobby for children's rights and involvement in society. But the existence of such campaigning illustrates the nature of this prevailing belief that children are passive, incomplete and dependent and they at all times need our care and our protection.

The second view is that children are increasingly out of control, disrespectful and delin-quent. We only need to get a selection of newspapers in any one week and watch both local and national news to see both these views manifested. We will see examples like 'brave' and 'suffering' children with terminal illnesses or disabilities; children as powerless victims of abuse or exploitation; anxiety-ridden parents who cannot let their children out of their sight lest a paedophile abduct them. And we will see other examples of aggressive 'hoodies', of bul-lying and gang culture, of drunken teenagers, shootings on the streets, 'happy slapping' and residents fearful of the 'local yobs'.

As Gill put it recently 'Adult anxieties typically focus on children's vulnerability, but they can also portray children as villains, again recasting normal childhood experiences as some-thing more sinister' (2008:11).

What we are far less likely to see and read about are the real stories of real children's lives and their actual achievements and genuine problems. Instead children themselves both get sentimentalized for their courage and diminished for their neediness, or they get blamed and vilified for their behaviours. As a result, society is successfully distracted from (a) hearing the real voices of everyday children and (b) facing the substantive and changing issues that affect children today. So we should not be surprised that children end up being perceived as an 'out-group' that is, inferior and not worthy of the same respect as adults.

Our view – based on both our life experiences of over half a century, where we have seen issues like sexism and racism come to the political and societal fore – is that children are the most oppressed group in society.

Reflection opportunity

Test this out for yourself. Ask a number of different people to list as many phrases or statements as they can, that they have heard adults over the years saying (a) to children and (b) about children.

When we have done this, nearly all the statements have been negative and even the positive ones were patronizing. There was also some comfortable laughter at many of the phrases. Can you imagine however, conducting the same exercise with the focus on some other societal or minority group and getting such an easy and overwhelmingly annulling response?

You may feel that we are painting too dark a picture and that we are ignoring political initiatives to improve children's lives such as the United Nations Convention for the Rights of the Child, or closer to home programmes like SureStart and Every Child Matters? Surely these represent real progress? We don't doubt there are lots of people with a genuine commitment to children's rights and participation and we know there are great and applaudable examples of good practice and some fantastic projects. But on the macro level, many good intentions at political level don't change attitudes on the ground and are also still coming from a superior perspective of what can and should be done *for* children. It is less often that we hear the rhetoric of true participation, working *with* children to effect change.

Consultation has been a buzzword in recent years and programmes to find out children's views have abounded. Sadly many of these have taken little account of the relationship between the consulting adult and the child 'consultee'. Unless this relationship is a truly equal one, where the adult genuinely listens and recognizes that children's perspectives differ from those of adults, consultation will be of no value, because the child will only say what the adult wants to hear – if she or he speaks at all.

Many of these consultations have also taken little account of who originated the topic and why and therefore the subject is almost always chosen by adults for adult reasons and may be of little or no interest or concern to children themselves. Perhaps the old adage of children being seen and not heard is not from a bygone age after all.

So here we are, nearing the end of a chapter entitled 'The Child' and yet all we have reviewed are adults' perspectives of children. What do children make of all this? How do they see themselves? While the adult world around them wrestles with how best to nurture them and/or discipline them, what do children say and feel about their lives?

Sociology of childhood

It is only relatively recently that sociologists have looked at the sociology of childhood itself and how children see themselves. Previous models viewed children as either passive (and therefore naturally integrated by adults into society) or potentially threatening (and therefore shaped by the adults in their lives and made-to-fit into society). Here again we see the same black-and-white views about children.

However, some sociologists have moved away from the idea that socialization is an individual process where the whole point is to grow up and become an adult. As Rich-Harris says 'a child's goal is not to become a successful adult, any more than a prisoner's goal is to become a successful guard. A child's goal is to be a successful child' (1998:198). Sociologists such as Corsaro (2005) and Mayall (2002) have looked at children as a social group existing in the present and see children negotiating, sharing and creating culture 'by creatively taking or appropriating information from the adult world to address their own peer concerns . . . they are not simply internalising society and culture but actively contributing to cultural production and change' (2005:18).

In other words, children are not just adults-in-the-making – their lives are valid and contributory throughout their childhood and they create their own rules and methods of communication that are different to adults, reflecting their different needs, interests and concerns while growing up. Rich-Harris admirably argues that children are not socialized and brought up by their parents, but by other children.

> Children are not incompetent members of the adult society: they are competent members of their own society, which has its own standards and culture. . . . loosely based on the majority adult culture within which it exists. But it adapts the majority adult culture to its own purposes and it includes elements that are lacking in the adult culture. And like all cultures, it is a joint production. (1998:199)

Children's free time with each other is highly prized and valued – they make 'persistent attempts to gain control of their lives and they always attempt to share that control with each other' (Corsaro, 2005:134).

Children are active players in their lives and they experience the world in a different way. If we are to work with and to understand children, we have to try and enter their world and see it through their eyes, for it is truly another place. It is helpful to be in touch with how we thought and felt as a child, but we must not assume that childhood is the same for each generation – it is not. When we come from a position of profound respect for children and a willingness to learn from them and about them, we will find that our conception of who they are also changes. We will find along with Malaguzzi that 'our image of the child is rich in potential, strong, powerful, competent and connected to adults and other children' (1993:10).

> ## Reflection opportunity
>
> What image do we find we personally hold of who children are and where does this come from? What was your image of yourself as a child? Do you think others saw you like this? Do you have the same image of your friends at the time? Thinking about children now – especially those you work with – what is your image of them? Is it the same or different to that you have of yourself and other children in the past? Which images are accurate and how do you know? Does the organization we work in influence this?

Reflection – Ali

I fostered for several years and at the same time did a lot of training around child abuse from children's perspectives for other carers, social workers, youthworkers and playworkers. I suddenly one day realized that I was beginning to see almost everyone as potentially abused or potential victims and that this was affecting the way I was relating to children and adults alike. I also was very shy as a child, had few friends and struggled with gaining social skills and a sense of self-esteem. This image of me as a child, coupled with the image of all children as vulnerable was actually skewing my whole world-view. I had to work quite hard at reframing this so that I had a more realistic image of people in general and children in particular.

So what do we in playwork make of all this? What is the 'right' image of children? What messages do we – consciously or unconsciously – give out to children about who they are? Certainly we need to have a holistic approach and set out to 'address the whole child; the child with body, mind, emotions, creativity, history and social identity. This is not the child only of emotions – the psychotherapeutic approach, nor only of the body – the medical approach, nor only of the mind, the traditional teaching approach' (Moss and Petrie, 2002:143). Do those of us in the playwork sector also need to add here – 'nor only of the child at play, the playwork approach? Do we sometimes focus so much on play that we lose sight of the whole child?

Perhaps of all available professional models, the pedagogical approach is the most relevant to playworkers and in fact it could be the basis for any professional working with children. The underlying principle of pedagogy is that children and adults are fundamentally equal but different and together embark on journeys to reflect and enquire and learn from and surprise one another – an interpersonal relationship that is both mutual and reciprocal. Pedagogues believe that a child is not an adult-in-waiting, but 'an active and creative actor, a subject and citizen with potentials, rights and responsibility . . . worth listening to and having a dialogue with and who has the courage to think and act by himself – a constructor in the construction of his own knowledge and his fellow being's common culture' (Dahlberg, 1997:22). If we really believe that – and it is absolutely in keeping with the Playwork Principles – and daily reflect on whether that belief is truly guiding what we say and do, we will have gone some way to seeing children as they are.

Further reading

Corsaro, W. (2005) 2nd edition. *The Sociology of Childhood*. London: Sage Publications.

Moss, P. and Petrie, P. (2002) *From Children's Services to Children's Spaces*. London: Routledge Falmer.

Palmer, S. (2006) *Toxic Childhood*. London: Orion.

Pringle, M. K. (1975) *The Needs of Children*. London: Routledge.

Prout, A. and James, A. (1977) Eds. *Constructing & Reconstructing Childhood*. London: Falmer Books.

Rich-Harris, J. (1998) *The Nurture Assumption*. New York: Touchstone.

Tucker, N. (1977) *What is a Child?* London: Open Books Publishing.

References

Argyris, C. & Schon, D. (see Wendy's article in *Therapeutic Playwork Reader*). Sheffield. Ludemos Associates.

Aries, P. (1962) *Centuries of Childhood*. New York: Vintage Books.

Bandura, A. (1977) *Social Learning Theory*. New York: General Learning Press.

Bowlby, J. (1969) *Attachment and Loss*. London: Institute of Psychoanalysis.

Bowlby, J. (1969) *Attachment and Loss: Vol 1 Attachment*. New York: Basic Books.

Brockliss, L. and Rousseau, G. (2003) *The History Child*. Oxford Magazine 0th week.

Bronfenbrenner, U. (1979) *The Ecology of Human Development: Experiments by Nature & Design*. Cambridge: Harvard University Press.

Bruner, J. S. (1986) *Actual Minds, Possible Worlds*. Cambridge, MA: Harvard University Press.

Burghardt, G. M. (2005) *The Genesis of Animal Play: Testing the Limits*. Cambridge, MA: The MIT Press.

Corsaro, W. (2005) 2nd edition, *The Sociology of Childhood*. London: Sage Publications.

Cunningham, H. (2006) *The Invention of Childhood*. BBC Books.

Dahlberg, G. (1997) 'The Child and the Pedagogue as Co-constructors of Culture and Knowledge' in *Voices about Swedish Childcare SoS Report*. Stockholm: Socialstyrelsen.

deMause, L. (1974) *The History of Childhood*. New York: The Psychohistory Press.

Erikson, E. (1950). *Childhood and Society*. New York: Norton.

Freud, S. (1914) *The Psychopathology of Everyday Life*. New York: Macmillan.

Gesell, A. (1943) *Infant and Child in the Culture of Today*. New York: Harper & Bros.

Gill, T. (2007) No Fear – *Growing Up in a Risk-averse Society*. London: Calouste Gulbenkian Foundation.

Groos, K. (1901) *The Play of Man*. New York: Appleton.

Hall, G. S. (1904) *Adolescence: Its Psychology and its Relations to Physiology, Anthropology, Sociology, Sex, Crime, Religion and Education* Vol. 1. New York: Appleton.

Hanawalt, B. A. (1993) *Growing Up in Medieval London: The Experience of Childhood in History*. New York: Oxford University Press.

Hughes, B. (2001) *Evolutionary Playwork and Reflective Analytic Practice*. London: Routledge.

King, M. T. (1934) *Mothercraft*. London: Simpkin, Marshall Ltd.

Leach, P. (1989) *Baby and Child*. Harmondsworth: Penguin.

Liedloff, J. (1975) *The Continuum Concept*. Harmondsworth: Penguin.

Lindon, J. (2007) *Understanding Children & Young People*. London: Hodder Arnold.

Magaluzzi, L. (1993) 'For an education based on relationships in young children' 11/93 p. 10. Washington DC.

Mayall, B. (2002) *Towards a Sociology for Childhood*. Buckingham: Open University Press.

Moss, P. and Petrie, P. (2002) *From Children's Services to Children's Spaces*. London: Routledge Falmer.

Nasaw (1985) *Children of the City: At Work and at Play*. New York: Anchor.

Palmer, S. (2006) *Toxic Childhood*. London: Orion.

Paul's first letter to the Corinthians Ch.13, v.12 (1804) in *The Holy Bible*. British and Foreign Bible Society.

Piaget, J. (1969) *The Psychology of the Child*. New York: Basic Books.

Pollock, L. (1983) *Forgotten Children: Parent-child Relations* 1500–1900. Cambridge: Cambridge University Press.

Postman, N. (1994) *The Disappearance of Childhood*. New York: Vintage Books.

Reaney, M. J. (1916) *The Psychology of the Organised Game*. Cambridge: Cambridge University Press.

Rich-Harris, J. (1998) *The Nurture Assumption*. New York: Touchstone.

Skinner, B. F. (1953) *Science and Human Behaviour*. New York : Macmillan.

Spock, B. (1945) *Baby & Child Care*. London: W. H. Allen & Co.

Stone, L. (1990) *The Family, Sex and Marriage in England 1500–1800*. Harmondsworth: Penguin Books.

Thomas, H. (1998–2009) Essay Series p1, www.elizabethi.org./uk/essays/childhood.htm

Vygotsky, L. S., van der Veer, R. & Valsiner, J. (1994) *The Vygotsky Reader*. Oxford: Blackwell.

Watson, J. B. (1970) *Behaviourism*. New York: W. W. Norton.

Wilber, K. (1996) *Up from Eden*. Wheaton, IL: Quest Books.

Young, J. Z. (1978) *Programs of the Brain*. Oxford: Oxford University Press.

In the previous chapters we have reflected on what playwork is and isn't; ideas that abound about play, and perceptions of 'the child'. In this chapter we will examine the actuality of the playworker's role in relation to the playing child. Before proceeding, the Playwork Principles (Chapter 1) and the complexity of theory surrounding play (Chapters 2 and 3) should be fully studied for we now come to look at what a playworker actually does, which is underpinned by these. What exactly is the main role of a playworker and how can it best be fulfilled? We will start by looking at the play environment and the playworker's role in relation to this and then continue with the other most important aspects of playwork namely: materials for play; observing children playing; and if, when and how to intervene when children are playing.

Some other parts of the playworker role will be considered in following chapters, where the necessity for the function emanates from legislation and the duty of care. These are an integral part of all work with children, but these aspects will also be examined with a play focus. From a playwork perspective it would seem impossible for any work with children to not involve play in some way, given that play is a major drive in children's lives. Leaving the potential for play out would seem like leaving out oxygen, the potential for breathing!

Reflection – Jacky

I remember way back in a previous life, when I was an art teacher in a secondary school, that the most successful lessons were also the most playful ones – play and creativity having strong links. Many years later this was born out by a chance meeting with a former pupil who remembered the good attention I had given him related to his 'psychedelic sprouts' that nobody else had seen any sense in. Indeed when I came across playwork as a potential direction to head into it seemed to make far more sense to me than teaching as play allowed for endless and internally motivated creativity and experimentation from which so much more can be learnt than from a narrow curriculum.

The playworker and the play environment

Playwork has been described as 'the specific act of affecting the whole environment with the deliberate intention of improving opportunities for play' as suggested by the Playwork Working Party of Playboard (1987:47). It would seem that one of the major roles of a playworker then is related to 'the environment'. The Playwork Principles (2005) take this a step further by suggesting that the playworker should 'support all children and young people in the creation of a space in which they can play' thereby taking the emphasis of creation of the environment away from the playworker and giving them a subsidiary role that is more in the service of children creating the environment – the playworker thus becomes a conduit for creation rather than a creator. The power rests with the children. *Best Play* (2000:7) describes this as an approach that they characterize as 'low intervention, high response, and a style which supports rather than directs the child'. The playworker acts as 'a channel of access to new materials and tools and is a stimulus to children to explore and learn'. Hughes (2001:81) describes playwork as 'the craft of appropriate intervention and modification in children's play' and he goes on to say that this involves 'the interaction of two of the most complex entities we know, the human child and the environment in which it plays'. Let us now consider that environment.

The play environment

The environment that best supports play includes both the physical and psychological environment. Indeed in *Play Environments a Question of Quality*, Hughes suggests that 'a play environment lives or dies on a daily basis from the ambience it has' and that this is 'directly related to the playworker's consideration of the ingredients which go to creating it'. Thus the playworker has a massively important role in ensuring that their own impact is not one that inhibits or constrains play but one that facilitates the play process.

In an academic paper Sturrock (2007:17) outlines some of what he calls the 'truth validities' of playwork in which he suggests that the playspace (or play environment) is a 'mediated area between the playing of the child/ren and the playing of the playwork practitioner'.

Here he introduces the notion that the playworker also plays within the play environment but that this playing should be consciously engaged in, and should be the conscious generator of insights and understanding on the part of the playworker; while the child plays unconsciously, during which s/he is unconsciously developing or as Sturrock puts it is 'being and becoming' and it is at this interface of playing that both the child and the playworker develop. He thus assigns a very important role to the playworker of being aware of, or 'witnessing' what it is that goes on for both her and for the child/ren during playing within the play environment. He believes that the sharing of insights with colleagues and the development of understanding that is generated through this process is fundamental to the role of the playworker. This is of course part of reflective practice the tenets of which run throughout this book (see Chapter 1 and later in this chapter).

We can hear those of you who are practicing playworkers saying at this point, so if my role is to enable children to create their own play environment by creating an ambience that facilitates this and to develop insights related to playing that I share with my colleagues, why is it that I spend so much time doing other things that seem unrelated? Well are they?

Reflection opportunity

Reflect on your day-to-day work under these headings:

1 Enable children to create their own play environment
2 Create a good atmosphere for play
3 Reflect on the play process alone and with others and respond to this.

How much of what you do relates to these three major aspects of your role?

Of course these are not the only things expected of you as there is much for you to know and do, however if very little of your job relates to the above perhaps your, or your manager's focus needs shifting.

Creating play environments

Ambience

How do we go about creating an environment that allows children to create their own environment? This can be split into two distinct areas, the physical environment and the psychological environment, or ambience – the feel of a place or situation. Let us start by thinking about the ambience.

Reflection opportunity

What sort of ambience do the following phrases bring to mind in relation to your life and your choices of how to spend your own free time? Try and apply them to an environment for children's play:

> Strict rules that limit your involvement
> A few, obviously fair, rules
> No say in what you can do
> Freedom to do what you want within the normal scope of being with others
> Cold and unfriendly
> Warm and welcoming
> Disinterested
> Interested
> Interfering – won't leave you alone
> Pay no attention to you even when you need it
> Limited
> Lots of potential
> Too busy to care about you
> Treat you like a nuisance
> Treat you like a friend on an equal footing
> Patronizing

For children to be able to play freely the environment has to feel right. If the environment does not feel right they may well play but it will probably not be the sort of play that is of any use to them for their 'being and becoming'. So what ambience is needed?

In our chapter on 'The Gentle Art of Agonism' (2006) we suggest that to create an effective affective environment for play, playworkers should try and ensure the following in relation to the feel of a place:

1 an overall ambience of welcome, acceptance, freedom and playfulness
2 awareness of children's moods and emotional baggage
3 not to be fazed by children's strong feelings and to have a supportive repertoire of both positive and playful responses when required
4 to be comfortable with authentically expressing and talking about their own feelings.

Hughes (1996:48) says that 'a friendly, usable and secure environment is absolutely essential for most children' and he suggests that playworkers can affect the ambience in many ways such as by 'being friendly and affectionate, being energetic, even eccentric' and it is important that playworkers are not seen as experts who demonstrate how to do things but as people interested in playing and experimenting with things themselves thereby highlighting the unbounded possibilities within the play space.

We have both been very lucky and have had the opportunity, through our various involvements within the playwork world, to visit, observe and/or work with a wide range of different types of play provisions. We would say that the biggest and most important factor in providing for children's play in a setting where adults have to be present is the atmosphere created by the playworkers. There may be fantastic physical potential for play but if the playworkers are strict, domineering, non-permissional, interfering, scary, or unfriendly, that potential will probably not be realized.

Here is a list of potential 'ambience indicators' that are taken from *Play Environments a Question of Quality* and may help you think about the atmosphere of your own play provision.

1 Caring (playworkers will help children if they get into difficulties or hurt themselves)
2 Trustworthy (children know that the playworkers will not let them down)
3 Empowering (children in charge of own behaviour and feel powerful)
4 Enjoyable (children can be natural and have fun without too many rules)
5 Friendly (all children feel welcome. The provision attracts children who may be marginalized in other circumstances)
6 Familiar (children feel a sense of place and belonging because the provision reflects their life)
7 Homely (a place where children can feel at home, keep warm and dry, make food etc.)
8 Multi-choice (lots of opportunities, and a place where children can choose what to do and whether to do anything at all)
9 Sharing (the playworkers don't behave as if they own the resources and environment)
10 Non-detrimental (causes no harm to children and the children understand that everybody has the right to be themselves without fear of ridicule)
11 Non-judgmental (children don't feel as if they are being judged all the time – differences are considered normal)
12 Non-petty (children not constantly being told off for trivial things and what rules there are, should only exist for good reason)
13 Alternative (different to home, school etc. Range of different opportunities and experiences. Compensatory)
14 Respectful (children treated as competent human beings)
15 Secure (secure from strangers, dogs etc. Entry and exits safe. Playworkers alert)
16 Safe (Health and safety guidelines followed properly)
17 Spacious (there's room for children to play how they want to without feeling cooped up and limited)
18 Sanctuary (somewhere where children feel safe from the rigours of life – truly the children's environment where other adults only access via the playworkers)
19 Useful (the provision has meaning for children)
20 Unthreatening (the place and playworkers do not feel dangerous – bullying, racist and sexist behaviour etc. is sensitively – even playfully – challenged)
21 Variable (changeable and flexible in line with children's ideas and play needs)
22 Sensitively supervised (distant supervision and minimal intervention, when asked for or really needed)

Reflection opportunity

Assess your environment for play against these indicators. How does it measure up? Are there other indicators that you feel are important? Discuss these and the ones above with colleagues. Can you improve the ambience of your setting, and if so how?

Physical environment

If the ambience is right you have gone a long way towards creating the right kind of environment for play, but what if the physical environment is impoverished? Many impoverished play environments can be seen, such as tarmac yards and broken down playgrounds and yet still children play in them. What does a 'good' play environment look like? What are the elements that go towards making a great place to play?

Reflection opportunity

Try to remember a special place where you used to play as a child. Try to remember what it was like. What did it look like? Where was it? Why was it good to play there? What was it about the place that enabled you to have a good play experience?

Reflection – Ali

I remember a section of rhododendron bushes in my local park that created a kind of open-plan 'tunnel of rooms'. You could get inside and see everyone outside but they couldn't see you. It was a haven, a hiding space and all manner of imaginative places at different times; most importantly it felt truly ours because no adults could get in there. I can remember a variety of feelings, especially the fear and then the exhilaration at escaping and hiding from the park-keeper! I went back there recently and was amazed to find that my 'tunnel' was so small – in my memory it was the width of a room and the length of a field!

Many places that cater for children and care for children seem to think that children need bright colours, special areas for particular activities, plastic – lots of plastic and safety surfacing. Why is this? Think of a stream on the moors with rocks, rushing water, trees and shrubs, mounds and mud. Think of a rainy day and a picnic in the bottom compartment of a bunk bed that's been made into a den with an old sheet. Think of a huge cardboard box. Think of the woods. Many children find these sorts of places ideal for playing in – but where are the bright colours, the plastic and the safety surfaces? When we provide for children we often think about things other than play. How will I keep the place clean? How will I keep the children from hurting themselves? How will I indicate that this is a special place for children, nothing like anything you see in real life, only in children's films and television? How can I keep everything in order and easy to store and clear away? How can I demonstrate that I've spent my money on resources that will last? Actually what we should be asking ourselves is 'where are the children and their need for play' in all these questions?

The basic quality assessment framework within *The First Claim* (2001:23) asks playworkers to assess their play environments by seeing whether it creates/enables children to play with what is called The Playwork Curriculum, with some examples of what this might mean in practice:–

1 Fire – barbecues, candles, fire-pits/bins, storm kettles
2 Water – paddling pools, hoses, swimming, damming streams, water fights
3 Air – kites, banners, wind chimes, paper planes, balloons, wind socks, zipline
4 Earth – clay, gardening, mud painting, digging, mud pies, bug hunting
5 Identity – face painting, dressing up, masks, photos, using mirrors, role-play
6 Concepts – discussions or play about death, peace, justice, crime, culture etc.
7 The senses – music, cooking, textures, lighting, perfumes/smells, colour etc.
8 A varied landscape – structures, platforms, ditches, quiet or hidden areas etc.
9 Materials – tools, sports equipment, inflatables, video, computer, pots and pans
10 Building – camps, den-making, taking equipment apart, trolley building
11 Change – redecorating, digging tunnels, murals, redesigning areas
12 Focuses – theme days, special events, visiting specialists, unusual equipment
13 Alternatives – trips, residentials, special clubs/classes, choices/options
14 Tools – hammers, saws, chisels, craft knives, nails, needles, spades, pliers etc.
15 Loose parts – crates, barrels, sheets, wheels, wood, tyres, bricks, vessels etc.
16 Risk – rope-swing, climbing, balancing, wrestling, jumping, DIY, fires, height

---

Reflection opportunity

Think about your own play environment. Does it give opportunities for such as those mentioned above? What does your provision enable children to do? How do you enable children to create their own play environment?

We took this a bit further with a colleague of ours and created an Affective Play Survey (2006:12–29) to give playworkers the opportunity to assess their play environments against a whole host of elements listed under the following broad areas and specifically intended to help people providing indoor areas that may not of themselves be enticing for play:

1 Varied lighting (why always neon? What about lamps, coloured bulbs etc . . . .?)
2 Different types of colours and tones created in different ways and by different means (consider paintwork, walls, ceilings, furniture, fabrics . . .)

3 Different types of images (of what? Of whom? Who chooses? . . .)
4 Different aromas (nice & nasty – anything other than antibacterial spray!)
5 Changeable layout with different heights, levels and slopes (indoors too)
6 Different and flexible types, shapes, sizes and uses of spaces
7 Different sounds at different levels of intensity (music, bird calls, trains, the sea, voices etc.)
8 Variety of comfort factors, such as variable temperatures, places to rest or chill out, places that might evoke expression of emotion or differing moods
9 Opportunities for ownership such as named cups, own cushion etc.
10 Sensory awareness of touch, sight, sound and smell
11 Availability and flexibility of all loose parts (where and how are they stored so that everybody can access them?)

Hughes (1996:33) asks us to consider why a child might be attracted to a play space. From asking children a series of questions he comes up with what he describes as 'content indicators'. These describe some of the things that children have indicated attract them to play and give us another set of tools for examining our play environment.

Reflection opportunity

Think about a play environment you know or work in. Could any of the words below be used to describe the environment and what it has to offer? What changes could be made to try and incorporate more of them?

- Absorbing
- Physically challenging
- Diverse
- Exciting
- Exhilarating
- Fun
- Exploratory
- Compensatory
- Interesting
- Magic
- Larger than life
- Malleable
- Child-scale
- Mysterious
- Permanence
- Private
- Relaxing
- Risky

The two words which best sum up what is important in the physical environment of a play space are flexibility and adaptability. Children have differing play needs at different stages of their childhood and at different times depending upon ambience, time of day, their mood, current circumstances, other people present, props available, risk taking needs (see Chapters 3 and 6 for more information on risk taking) etc. A place that has been specifically designated as a place for children to play therefore has to take account of all these factors and for the fact that it will be used by lots of different children all with their own variable and differing needs. Those needs can only be guessed at by witnessing, reflection and IMEE (2001:22) which is a simple reflective tool which helps playworkers to analyse the quality of their play environment against their intuition (what do I think makes a good play environment?), memory (of their own good childhood play environments), experience (from their own professional practice) and evidence (from the scientific literature) and even when you have been through this process you may not begin to guess what children have in their own minds.

Reflection opportunity

Think back to the special places you liked to play in as a child. In what way were they adaptable and flexible? How did you use that potential?

Reflection – Jacky

I remember a large cupboard on the landing, filled with old bits of furniture, luggage etc. outside my parents' bedroom. 'My friends and I took it over for our own use, with the unspoken knowledge of my mum and dad. It was variably, a club house, a shop, a hiding place, a place to talk secrets where nobody else could hear you, a witches coven, a place to do the Ouija board, and a place of interest to sort through old stuff and wonder about it. Most particularly it felt like a place that had masses of potential that we felt grown ups would overlook. For them it was a storage place for life's junk.'

Reflection – Ali

I recall recently reflecting with a colleague on what children had called specific physical areas in a playcentre over a period of time and noting these down. A 'corridor' round the back of the building had been a chicane, a race-track, a gully, a tunnel, a prison, a kennel and a petrol station. The ditch and shrubs round the perimeter of the outside space had been the centre of the earth, the ravine, the jungle, the place where the monsters live under our power, the rumbling volcano, and 'our' camp. The climbing frame had been the circus, the mountain, the tent and the obstacle course. The sandpit had been the desert and the temple of doom. The mats indoors had been islands, wrestling rings, houses and stepping stones. A corner had been a den, a cave and a shelter.

A designated play place should be seen as a 'compensatory' environment, one which is compensating for the fact that much of our modern life in the West and particularly in Britain, does not take account of the play needs children have. The outside world is dominated by the rush of traffic, people in a hurry to get to and from where they are going (for many middle-class children that is in a car and going to and from organized activities and classes), consumer-orientated local areas where touching of goods is forbidden unless you are buying, vast tracts of concrete, fear of strangers and abduction, fear of children and young people and lack of community interest. For some children the outside world is their playground and without the interest of adults they can and do cause problems for themselves and for others.

The inside world for many children after they have finished any chores they may have to do, consists of passive entertainment or educational activity, a plea for keeping things clean, tidy and quiet and if they play to play with their toys in a sensible manner. Many parents have neither the time nor energy for involving themselves with their children's play and many others are too controlling and never allow their children time and space to play on their own and in their own way. For some children, where perhaps they are the breadwinner or the carer, there is not even time to play.

The role of the adult in playwork is to enable the child to play freely in the play environment. This is rather well described in an extract about play provision provided for children who visit Wakefield Prison.

> The child needs to feel free in order to play freely. For this the child needs to feel welcome and secure. Play takes place within a frame which sets it apart from the adult world and it is possible that the presence of an adult who is sympathetic but not involved in the child's play may serve to reinforce the child's sense of being apart from the adult world when it is at play. The playworker gives a sort of licence to play by serving as a presence which can indicate the boundaries of what is permissible. The child's play can be regarded as an attempt to retain personal freedom and control in the face of the demand to adjust to conventional norms. (Tamminen, B. and Chown, S., 2000)

Resources and materials for play

Children will play anywhere and with anything that is usable for play if they have time and inclination – let us take an example, such as a six-foot wall surrounding an unused piece of land that is intended to keep trespassers out. This is a potential play magnet for lively minds and gives opportunity for such things as the following: playing ball against; a home base in tag; graffiti surface; surface to stick things on; brick counting opportunity; climbing on (with or without help) and jumping off; climbing over as before; walking along; meeting place; or a destruction opportunity.

> **Key question**
>
> Can you think of any more?

We often mainly think of toys and games when we consider resources for play because these are obviously designed specifically for children and they are very heavily marketed. Children

Photo 5.1 Ball needs wall?

and adults are equally prey to sales techniques and we are all attracted to new and novel products. However when we think deeply about play we realize that children don't so much need 'things' as they need 'potential'. It is important then to consider which things or types of things have the most potential for play.

Key question

Consider the following items and using IMEE as your starting point, list all the potential for play that you can think of associated with each play resource, separately or together:

1 two sheets
2 pack of cards
3 pull along dog
4 cans
5 stones
6 barrel
7 washing line and pegs
8 doll

You can do this exercise with any number of items.

> ### Reflection – Jacky
>
> I remember at various times in my life as both a child and adult, with and without others, spending considerable amounts of time building card houses, throwing stones into or at old cans, and practising different types of knots. I gained a great deal of satisfaction from the odd and accidental height of a card house, hitting of can or slipping of knot, but equally just as much frustration from all my failures (measured against whatever I or other players designated to be a success).
>
>   Sometimes the motivation for this activity was the potential onset of boredom or having no specific purpose to a period of time other than being and not feeling pressurized to do something purposeful, sometimes it was because a desire to throw stones or whatever would just come over me, sometimes it was to do something collectively and sometimes it was initiated to fill in time between planned activities. However I would now, as an adult and playworker, based on my own memory, be able to pretend to somebody who pressurized me into designating all play opportunities on offer with a recognized outcome, that the offering of 'stones, cans, and a washing line' would help with physical, intellectual, emotional, creative and social development and that it would offer opportunity for the following play types to be engaged in:– exploratory; object; social; and creative. I of course would have no idea whether this would be the case as another child or children playing with the same play resources may play differently, develop different aspects of their being, may engage in different play types or may choose not to play with these things at all.

Shelley Newstead (2004:28) talks about 'play value' or the cardboard box theory. In other words children can usually get more play out of the cardboard box that a toy comes in, than in the toy itself. Children like to have stuff to play with when the motivation to play comes upon them.

> ### Reflection – Jacky
>
> I remember a boy who came to the after-school club I ran, who mainly liked to play alone. He had made himself a shield, helmet and sword out of cardboard and a mobile castle out of a large cardboard box. During a period of about 3 weeks David would set his castle up every afternoon, either indoors or outdoors (depending upon the rain factor and cardboard) and he then spent the evening defending his castle against potential marauders, of whom there were occasionally a few and but often none. When the 'coast was clear' (which was most of the time) he would sit in his castle coming out only for snack or to make minor adjustments to his castle. Every evening when he went home he would ask us playworkers to keep his castle safe until the next day. Eventually one evening he said 'I don't want this any more' and gave it back to us. We offered it to others but by then nobody else wanted it either.

When is a play resource not a play resource then? When it is not played with or when it is not played with in the way that an adult thinks it should be played with or when an adult decides that it is not a play resource?

   This does not mean, of course, that there are no boundaries to the way that any play resource can be used. Playwork occurs in the real world and therefore much play behaviour is unacceptable to many people. Throwing stones at a can when the stone and the can are not near glass windows or other people etc. is fine but if you were an adult present during a stone-throwing game you may feel impelled to intervene if for instance you saw that the chances of a child breaking a window were very high, if only in order to prevent the child getting into trouble.

Play resources then could be seen as anything made available for children to play with that has play value. The more flexible and adaptable the resource is and the more it can be combined with other resources, the better for play. Availability and usability are vital. Children's understanding of, and freedom to choose, what, how, when, where, they can play with the resources in a play environment, will be communicated by playworkers who have created a 'permissional' ambience that caters for free play, where children are in charge of the content and intent of their play. The only limiting factor will be what resources there are, not how the resources can be used. The constant topping up of play resources, in order to offer novel and stimulating potential for play is an important part of the playworker's role. Keeping alert to the potential for 'good' scrap is a skill well worth developing. Below is a list of some play resources under different headings that are well worth considering and collecting.

Natural – water, conkers, insects, stones, pebbles, sand, leaves, wind, mud, fur, seeds, rain, fire, straw/hay, seaweed, soil, coal, fir cones, shells, wax, flowers, snow/ice, fungi, acorns, sunlight, bugs, worms, feathers, berries, seeds, dust, ashes, rocks, animals, grass . . .

Paper – cardboard boxes/sheets, cards, loo rolls, newspaper, magazines, egg boxes, tissue, carpet tubes, paper cups/plates, frieze paper, wrapping paper, glitter, lining paper, wallpaper, tracing paper, rice paper, sweet wrappers, papyrus, corrugated paper, catalogues, shredded paper, scrap paper, crepe paper, hemp, toilet paper, sandpaper, risler papers . . .

Plastics – carrier bags, yoghurt pots, milk crates, bin liners, bubble wrap, tarpaulins, barrels, milk cartons, wrappings, straws, shoes, inflatables, moulds, Perspex, storage boxes, film canisters, trays, crisp packets, lino, bread crates, cups, cotton reels, polystyrene, sheeting, pipes/gutters, butts, bottles, buttons, beads, cellophane, cutlery, spatulas, acetate sheets . . .

Metal – bottle tops, pots/pans, tin cans, containers, magnets, trolleys, paper clips, nails, chains, keys/rings, car shells, wire, curtain rings, circuit boards, baking trays, old cutlery, chicken wire, coat hangers, dustbins, shovels, bike frames, zips, padlocks, ball bearings, handcuffs, gold/silver leaf, springs, wire wool, silver foil, coins, wheels, machine drums, CDs, tent pegs . . .

Fabrics – clothes, netting, sheets, silk, leather, string, football kits, bibs, cotton wool, blankets, tents, sacking, hats, jersey strips, velvet, curtains, aprons, rugs, carpets, felt, cushions, wool, parachutes, canvas, tights, socks, cargo nets, hammocks, seatbelts . . .

Rubber – tyres, hose, gloves, wellies, shoe soles, balls, inner tubes, elastic bands, matting, erasers, mats, tubing . . .

Wood – logs, pallets, garden canes, withies, poles, boarding, sawdust, branches, telegraph poles, driftwood, sticks, twigs, bamboo, planks, posts, benches, doors, frames, matches, boxes, crates, railway sleepers

Food (for cooking or creativity) – flour, pastas, lentils, potatoes, eggs, rice, cereals, chocolate, breads, onions, fruits, herbs, spices, food colouring, salt dough, cornflour, compost, icing sugar, pumpkins, vegetables, nuts, beans/pulses, jelly, coffee, custard, twiglets . . .

Vessels – jars, cups, bowls, buckets, trunks, butts, skips, bottles, boxes, watering cans, jugs, plant pots, sponges, baskets, oil drums, pods, crates, baths, window boxes, guttering/downpipes, rucksacks, sacks . . .

Objects – chairs/sofas, tables, wheelbarrows, torches, trolleys, bricks, clothes horses, breeze blocks, incinerator bins, brooms, stage blocks, wheels, fans (to create wind), hay/straw bales, large cable reels, mattresses, crash mats, bikes, prams, coffin, nets, boat . . .

Photo 5.2 Hooray for loose parts!

Tools – hammers, screws, screwdrivers, nails, saws, nuts/bolts, tape, needles, drills, measures, chisels, cutters, rollers, staplers, sieves, staple guns, scissors, drawing pins, hoes, brushes, rakes, pliers, knives, string/rope, forks, hole punch, spades, matches, mallet, markers, chainsaw, glue, crowbar, pegs, axe, clips, pick axe, dibber, blutac, spirit level, grips . . .

Identity – wigs, hats, shoes, glasses, uniforms, make-up, jewellery, belts, cloaks, scarves, shawls, masks, sunglasses, cameras, puppets, dressing up clothes, face paints, henna, hair accessories, fake tattoos, flags, religious symbols, large pieces of material, cultural props, books/pictures of diverse people . . .

If storage is a problem we have to find some way of overcoming that problem. How about portable storage boxes; stacking boxes; hammocks or hanging baskets that can be hung above the space; trolleys that can be wheeled away; or an outside storage hut? The play needs of children are important and as 'advocates' for play we have a duty to use our own power, creativity and imagination to solve those things which interfere with our ability to provide for play.

Observation in playwork

The best way of learning about children and their play is to observe, and listen to, children when they are playing. Children are the experts in their own play and can teach you much. However in order to learn from them you have to learn to concentrate, observe

Photo 5.3 Testing self.

with your eyes and ears and with an open mind. This takes time and skill and requires practice. If you approach the task thinking that you already know what you are going to see and hear, you will learn little or nothing. For observation to be worthwhile it must be approached with an enquiring mind. Almost all theories related to children, their play and how it links to development, learning, health etc. have been developed through observation.

You can try asking children written or oral questions about their play but what you will often get from this is answers to questions. Play, as a form of behaviour, is a far more truthful medium of communication and will 'leak' all sorts of information. Once you have collected the information through observation, it has to be analysed and interpreted against other information that has been gained through the IMEE reflective process in order for it to be useful.

Some people use playful techniques for consulting and involving children, particularly when wanting to gain their views about play. Methods such as taking photographs of favourite places in the setting, sticking smiley or scowling faces onto pictures of particular pieces of equipment, drawing favourite activities etc. can be used, and sometimes to good effect. However this should always be backed up with observational evidence. There is nothing as successful as non-intrusive observation of children playing for gaining information from children about their play.

Reflection opportunity

It is useful to practise being observant. This will require you to make some time to stand back and watch a chosen aspect of play such as:– specific children or a child playing; a particular playworker and child playing; a particular piece of equipment or area of the play space being used; a set or organized activity such as snack time, and concentrate on what you are seeing and hearing. First for a couple of minutes and gradually increasing the time so that you are training yourself to become more aware of what is going on and to build up your memory and a repertoire of knowledge which will inform your practice. Children may try to engage you in some way and you will need to find ways (playfully and respectfully!) to deal with this.

Take 5 minutes time out and spend a few moments in the middle of a session at your setting and observe what children are doing in a particular part of the play space. What types of play are happening? How are the children using the space and or the materials? How many children are involved? How many boys and or girls? What is the level of involvement? At the end of the session, try to recall as much information as possible. How much can you remember?

For certain types of information that you may wish to gain from the setting, such as how children 'feel' about aspects of the provision, you can attempt to be a 'participant observer' where you are going about your playworker role but covertly, observing things that happen, listening to what's being said and asking associated questions over a period of time. This requires you to have a good memory and there is the potential problem of 'contamination', that is, that your own participation in some ways influences how the child or children behave and feel, and therefore gives a false reading of a situation. This is easier to do if you are using a minimal intervention style, or can be classed as supernumery. If you behave in a 'minimally adult' way you are less likely to affect the way that the child/ren play and how they feel. In order to be useful, the information gained will have to be recorded in some way such as a reflective log so that it can be thought about and shared with colleagues.

Reflection opportunity

Choose some aspect of your provision that occurs on a regular basis and that you are also involved in, that might be interesting to find out about such as playing physical or imaginative games. Try to observe and listen to what children are doing and saying during this on a few different occasions. Ask non-obtrusive questions related to this, maybe about the characters most preferred or competitive versus co-operative games and keep a log of information based on all that you have found out. After a period of time analyse this information and see if you have learnt anything. Share this information with colleagues.

Sometimes you may feel that more formal observation is required. This could be for a number of reasons such as:

1 to better understand the play cues of a particular child
2 to see whether a particular layout of the play space is giving the best opportunities for children to play
3 to identify the play needs of a group of new children
4 to evaluate the setting, the involvement of playworkers etc.
5 to identify which play types are being manifested in the setting
6 to identify a particular child's play needs in relation to their development.

We have both had much opportunity to observe that which goes on in play settings related to quality assessment of the playwork practice. These observations have been guided by specific criteria that focus the mind of the observer. These observations have always been fascinating and often throw up both positive and negative information that the playwork practitioner has been unaware of, such as intuitively wonderful responses to the play cues of children but also adulterative responses that have spoiled the moment. Novel use of play resources by children free to play but also preconceived expectation by playworkers related to the use of certain resources. Only through observation can the minutiae of practice be examined in an objective manner and discussed with playworkers against their own reflection.

There are a number of different techniques for recording observations such as:

1 Narrative format. Everything seen and heard is recorded ongoing
2 Pre-designed form in written format, for example, speech and behaviour recorded separately
3 Time schedule where observations recorded at certain times throughout a period of time. Say every 15 minutes for 5 minutes
4 Tracking diagram where layout of area is pre-drawn and child's movement or a loose part is tracked with a line moving from place to place
5 Checklist – where a list of certain types of potential behaviour are pre-recorded and then ticked if seen.

There are also a number of things you need to consider if you are going to make formal recordings of your observation:

1 The ethics of observation – are you observing for good reason? Do you have the permission of the child/ren or parents to use information gained from observation? How will the information gained be used? What will you do if your observation inadvertently raises some concerns about the welfare of a child or the practice of a playworker?
2 Confidentiality – How will the observations be recorded and stored? Who will have access to the observations and the information that comes from them?
3 Do you have the time to observe? Do you have the support of your colleagues?
4 Do you have good reason to observe? What is the aim of observing?

5 Do you have the skill to observe and record information simultaneously? What method of observation will you use? How are you going to record the information that you gain? How are you going to handle interruptions?

In order to be aware of all influences on that which you are observing, all formal observation should contain some of the following information depending upon the aim:

1 details of context
2 time
3 place
4 numbers of children and adults present
5 genders, ethnicity, ability etc. if relevant
6 weather
7 materials and equipment available
8 layout of space
9 organization at time
10 time taken on observation
11 aim of observation

Reflection opportunity

Plan to carry out a formal observation and plan the time to do it. Choose four play types that you can easily recognize. Prepare an observation sheet divided into four sections with the name of a play type at the top of each one. Find a place to sit that is away from the action but enables you to see what is going on either in the whole setting or in one part. (Match the play types chosen to those you would most expect to see.) Observe for 10 or 15 minutes and record any examples of the play types seen in the appropriate area. Try to give detail of age, gender and activity for each recording. Develop shorthand if it will help.

Write the observation up more clearly if necessary and when you have the time consider what you can glean from the information you have recorded. Ask yourself questions such as: which play type was engaged in the most and why? Did boys and girls engage in the same or different play types? If children were playing together were they engaged in the same play type? Was the play type influenced by the materials/environment and if so how? How often, if at all did a child change the play type s/he was engaged in over the period of observation?

Approaches to intervention

Intervention is about the 'why, when and how' of playworkers engagement with children in the play environment and is at the heart of playwork practice. Of course all modification of the play environment and the very presence of playworkers is a form of intervention, but in this section we will mainly consider the actual involvement of playworkers during play sessions. Non-playwork people sometimes have difficulty with the minimal intervention approach of playwork, believing that they as adults can help a child 'learn' from his or her play experiences by their interventions. If children are the experts in their own play, and are in charge of it, this of course is not the case and much involvement can be seen as interference. When children play they learn from their own mistakes, successes and failures, and their own experiments. If a child is in charge of the content and intent of his or her own play, then missing out on the failures will have a negative developmental effect.

Intervention styles

The First Claim framework for quality assessment (2001:28) focuses the playworker on 'appropriate' playwork intervention styles which are essentially 'non-interventionist' and indicated by instructions so these styles are positive ways of intervening by mainly not intervening:

1 Wait to be invited to play
2 Enable play to occur un-interrupted by me
3 Enable children to explore their own values
4 Leave children to improve their own performance
5 Leave the content/intent of play to the children
6 Let children decide why they play
7 Enable children to decide what is appropriate behaviour
8 Only organize when children want me to.

Range of intervention

Sturrock et al. (2004:15–17) suggest that adult intervention in children's play should be only to facilitate the process, 'to extend the play they engage in, or to help children avoid imminent and serious harm to themselves and others.' They define four interventions which range from minimal to complex as follows:

1 Play maintenance – The play is self-contained – no intervention is necessary, the worker observes.
2 Simple involvement – The adult acts as a resource for the play. For example making a tool available.
3 Medial intervention – At the request of the child the adult becomes involved in the play (and withdraws as soon as is appropriate). For example initiates a particular game.
4 Complex intervention – There is a direct and extended overlap between playing children and the worker – the adult takes on a role in the play, or acts as a partner to the playing child. For example takes on a character as part of socio-dramatic play.

This range still concentrates on intervention as a method of helping the child have a better play experience, not intervention related to modifying the behaviour of children.

Wherever possible when a worker decides to intervene, their response should be playful, rather than controlling or prescriptive. There are of course times when it will be necessary for an intervention to not be playful. However this will be because it is not about play, but about the duty of care. The playworker's prime focus is the playing child and the playful process and this should take precedence whenever possible.

Intervention modes

The First Claim – Desirable Processes (2002) goes further and describes nine intervention 'modes' in some detail, giving descriptions of the circumstances that indicate use of a particular mode, how to intervene according to that mode and what the expected outcome of its use might be. In summary these are as follows:

1 Distance – The playworker keeps his/her distance, listens and watches without overtly looking. This mode is used for general supervision. Children feel free.
2 Perceived Authentic – The playworker behaves naturally engaging with the children and the play space in a non-adulterating way. Children perceive playworker as an honorary child and play in a non-adulterated way.
3 Without preconceptions – The playworker is totally focused on children's play processes and does not bring other adult agenda issues into the play space. To be used when other social, political, cultural or educational agendas are potentially being imposed. Children's total playtime is dedicated to playing.
4 Un-adulterating – The playworker only engages when invited or when responding to a child-initiated enquiry. Children feel responsible for their own actions and consequences.
5 Permissional – By engaging in them the playworker conveys to children that certain, often disapproved of, ways of being are permitted. Children feel comfortable to engage freely in play modes that might otherwise open them to ridicule or risk.
6 De-centred – The playworker observes in an analytical and diagnostic way in certain situations where children's emotions or behaviours need possible curative strategies. What can be done from a playwork perspective? It is play as therapy. Children feel increasingly comfortable and less disturbed as the situation is dealt with effectively.
7 Perceived indifferent – The playworker deliberately ignores certain targeted children. Used when a child is traumatized and needs a comfortable physical and psychological distance from the adult in order to heal him or herself. These children feel unmonitored and engage in play with the environment and peers in an unselfconscious, natural and spontaneous manner. Thus enabling play to do its work.
8 Without Stereotypical Play Narratives (SPNs) – The playworker does not have any expected/allowed games, narratives, behaviours which are imposed or enforced on the children. Children cannot be behaviourally blackmailed because of the circumstances they are in. To be used where adult pre-conceptions about the play setting are highly influencing. Children will feel relaxed, empowered and in control. Their relationship with the playworker will be joyful and happy.
9 Compensatory – The playworkers analyse the children's socio-economic and geographic context and try to compensate for any play deficits that may be resulting by providing a play environment and ambience that supports a comprehensive play experience. Children feel greater well-being and more at ease as the range and depth of their play experience increases.

Adulteration

Some playworker intervention says more about the playworker than it does about the playing child. Some playworkers have a lot of their own reactions to deal with and find it difficult not to become involved. When adults 'spoil' the meaning of children's play we can see this as a form of 'adulteration'.

Reflection – Ali

I remember a recent incident on a local open access playscheme. Two girls about ten years old who were best friends and had seemed inseparable, were standing near me when I heard one say suddenly to the other 'this best friend thing – sorry but it's just not working' and then she walked off arm in arm with another girl. The 'abandoned' girl – I'll call her Sara – stood there for a few minutes and then crawled into a den they had made that morning and didn't come out. After about half an hour I knelt at the den entrance and asked if she was okay. She had clearly been crying. I said I remembered how it felt when these things happen and that I was sorry and left her to come out when she felt ready. Some time later she did come out and involved herself with something else. The girl she had been friends with then came by with her new friend and Sara made some caustic comment I couldn't hear – the other girl then said 'Oooh, what's got into you?' in a mocking sing-song voice. I found myself saying, 'well you were pretty foul to her earlier' whereupon she stomped off arm in arm with a new friend. I thought no more of this and went off myself to get a cuppa. When I returned it seemed that war had broken out – Sara had gone for the other girl and they were now really scrapping on the grass with a crowd around them egging them on. I broke it up and all eventually settled down but the conversations afterwards and my reflections on my own words and feelings made me realize that what I had said to each of them earlier was triggered by my own memories of feeling dumped and excluded and so was loaded with unhelpful permissions and judgements that actually made Sara feel justified in attacking the other girl. I had reacted out of my own need to protect and rescue Sara, rather than respond to Sara herself.

Reflection opportunity

Can you see or hear yourself in any of the examples above and below?

Playworkers all have their own 'bête noires' of behaviour that unconsciously prompt an inappropriate or adulterative response – often as a result of their own past experiences or upbringing, for example, an accident in childhood; getting into trouble for untidiness; concern about what other people think, etc.

Some of us will find it is over safety – we find ourselves wanting to overprotect children when they need to learn to assess and cope with risk for themselves. 'You two are too little to be trying to carry that plank. We don't want you to drop it on your toes or hurt yourselves doing it, do we?' 'You are going to fall if you climb any higher. Watch where you're putting your feet on the way down or you could slip.'

Reflection – Jacky

I certainly have a problem with this one and find it very difficult to keep my mouth shut when children are doing risky things. For instance during a playscheme I was holding down a tarpaulin, that children were sliding down a slope on and that had come adrift from its peg. The tarpaulin had first been squirted with bubble bath and water and the children were having a wonderful time taking long run-ups and then throwing themselves down it, sometimes in great swathes and with whoops of joy. There was a melee of children's arms, legs and bodies sliding down before me and I heard myself shouting, 'Watch out, someone's going to get hurt'. This was a totally redundant exclamation that had no purpose and may have made some children expect to get hurt. The children were already on the very slippery slope and couldn't stop their movements even if they wanted to and nobody did get hurt. However because of concerns related to broken limbs, we playworkers stopped the action momentarily and we and the children did a quick risk assessment which resulted in them keeping their sliding group sizes smaller which seemed just as much fun but was safer and also resulted in one little girl who had declared that she did not do sliding feeling safe enough to have several goes.

Some others of us will feel we need to make sure everyone is happy and so we try to sort out every child's problems so that they have no reason to feel miserable, when it is perfectly normal to feel unhappy at times. 'You need to put a coat on if you're going out. It's freezing. Here, I'll get it for you.' 'I can see you are having difficulty with sticking those two boxes together. Shall I do it for you?'

Others of us find that certain behaviours or attitudes irritate us, or make us anxious, so we over control behaviour or remonstrate with children when they need to explore their own effects and boundaries. 'This can only end in tears. You two stop squabbling over that. Try and play nicely together.' 'There are rules to this game. Listen! I said Listen! I'll tell you what they are to make sure that you all play properly; otherwise things will just get out of hand.'

Still others of us feel that we have a lot to offer children and so we often find ourselves 'teaching' – unnecessarily passing on skills and information when it is not asked for and which can crush children's own curiosity and creativity. 'Nice painting Maddy but to make a proper green for the grass you need to add more yellow. Why don't you try dabbing the paint on with a sponge to give it more texture?'

And many of us still have 'un-played-out material' so we want to play and be in charge of the play, rather than support the children's play. 'Let me have a go first to see what it's like. Oh great! It's jolly good fun! To get the best experience you need to slide down the left side. Let me have another go.' 'We're all going to add something to the mural but it needs to look good so I've drawn in the outlines first and pencilled in what colour they need to be.'

The examples given are some of the most common adulterative responses and many of us will find we can identify with some, if not all! There are however, various and more complex forms of each and it is only through reflective practice that we can discover which ones affect us most. Is it to help; to rescue; to organize; to control; to care; to teach?

Where adulteration occurs, 'the frame of the child's play is entirely polluted by the playworker's conscious or unconscious wishes and desires.' It is therefore really important that playworkers become increasingly aware of their impact in a play space.

As Crowe says 'we have so trivialized play and tried to confine it to the "proper" time and place with "proper" toys, or manipulated it for so-called educational ends, that we no longer see or recognize it as part of the life-force itself' (1983:27).

Times when intervention is required

There are of course, times when 'intervention' is appropriate as follows:

1 Child initiated – When a child 'invites' intervention either overtly, by asking for help or interaction with a playworker, or less obviously by non-verbal communication and the issuing of a play cue.
2 Child distressed – When a child is clearly upset or unhappy and the playworker perceives that comfort and support is required.
3 Child has extra support needs – When a child has a condition as previously recognized and requires support in specific situations or in relation to issued play cues.
4 Children in dispute – When a disagreement or argument has escalated beyond the point at which the children can handle it for themselves.
5 Children engaged in violent behaviour – When behaviour becomes dangerous or very destructive.

The timing of intervention is always a judgement call. Too early an intervention can sometimes result in 'adulteration' of the play, or to the creation of an atmosphere that is not conducive to playing. Too late an intervention can lead to frustration on the part of a child, problem behaviour getting out of control or the children's perception that the playworkers are of no use to them. As playworkers we need to consciously think about the ways in which we do and don't intervene and interact with children (and why we do) in order to see if these match up with the styles and modes listed above. We also need to be able to talk about what we do and don't say and do with our colleagues – this takes honesty and courage, but often our colleagues will be able to see the impact we have (for better or worse!) more easily than we can. Reflective practice is vital in relation to intervention so that the playworker can also learn and develop through his or her, own experiences as matched against the knowledge and experience of others.

In this chapter we have considered the primary roles of a playworker, namely to: create an appropriate physical and psychological environment for play; to observe children playing and to reflect on this using a range of different reflective techniques; to be aware of a range of different approaches to intervention and use the most appropriate one in each different circumstance; to be aware of the effects that our own intervention can have on the playing child. In the following chapter we look at some further roles of the playworker that are less directly related to play.

Further reading

Hughes, B. (1996) *Play Environments: A Question of Quality*. London: Playlink.

Kilvington, J. Wood, A. and Knight, H. (2006) 'Affective Play Spaces' Unpublished paper presented at *New Directions in Children's Geographies Conference*, Northampton University, 2006.

Newstead, S. (2004) *The Buskers Guide to Playwork*. Eastleigh: Common Threads.

NPFA (2000) *Best Play what Play Provision Should Do for Children*. London: National Playing Fields Association.

Wood, A. (2005) *Playwork Resources*. Solihull: Handout Building Blocks.

Wood, A. and Kilvington, J. (2007) 'The Gentle Art of Agonism – Speculations and Possibilities of Missing Female Perspectives in Playwork Theory' in Russell, W. Handscomb, B. and Fitzpatrick, J. (Eds) *Playwork Voices in Celebration of Bob Hughes and Gordon Sturrock:* The London Centre for Playwork Education and Training.

References

Building Blocks (2005) *Reflective Practice*. Handout for Playwork Level 3 Occupational Standards Training Day. Solihull.

Crowe, B. (1983) '*Play is a Feeling*'. London: George Allen & Unwin.

Hughes, B. (1996) *Play Environments: A Question of Quality*. London: Playlink.

Hughes, B. (2001) *Evolutionary Playwork and Reflective Analytic Practice* London and New York: Routledge.

Hughes, B. (2001) *The First Claim*. Cardiff: Play Wales.

Hughes, B. (2002) *The First Claim . . . . .Desirable Processes*. Cardiff: Play Wales.

Newstead, S. (2004) *The Buskers Guide to Playwork*. Eastleigh: Common Threads.

NPFA (2000) *Best Play what Play Provision Should Do for Children*. London: National Playing Fields Association.

Playboard (1987) *Neighbourhood Playwork Training Scheme – Pilot Project 2 – Resource Pack*. Cardiff: Playboard.

Playwork Principles. Play Principles Scrutiny Group (2005) *Playwork Principles*. Cardiff: Play Wales.

Sturrock, G. (2007) 'Towards Tenets of Playwork Practice' in *Ip Dip* 1, 17 (Meynell Games).

Sturrock, G. and Else, P. (1998) *The Colorado Paper – The Playground as Therapeutic Space: Playwork as Healing*. Sheffield: Ludemos Associates.

Sturrock, G. Russell, W. Else, P. (2004) *Towards Ludogogy: The Art of Being and Becoming through Play. The Birmingham Paper*. Sheffield: Ludemos Associates.

Tamminen, B. and Chown, S. (2000) 'Behind Bars: Children's Experience of Visiting the Play Facility at Wakefield Prison'. *New Playwork – New thinking*. Ely: The Proceedings of PlayEducation 2000.

Playwork Regulation 6

In Chapter 5 we identified the main aspects of a playworker's role, as underpinned by The Playwork Principles. Now we look at how legislation and some external systems impact on playwork and thus the role of the playworker. We will also look at how playwork in turn puts its own stamp on these.

An important part of being a playworker is to know, understand and apply all the relevant legislation that applies to your work. Laws, regulations and the way that they are put into practice change all the time. Where legal aspects are mentioned in this chapter they are current as at the date of writing, however it is the responsibility of the reader to check the latest situation and to ensure that information is up to date.

At the end of the chapter there are websites and references to cover the issues highlighted here and other relevant legislation and information.

UK Governments and regulation of playwork

The United Kingdom is made up of four separate countries; England, Scotland, Wales and Northern Ireland. The UK Government runs in England, but Scotland, Wales and Northern Ireland have their own Governments and devolved administrations: the Scottish Parliament, the National Assembly for Wales and the Northern Ireland Assembly. There is a different relationship and different levels of power and responsibility between the

UK Government and each of the other three administrations. Many laws that are passed by the UK Government are relevant to all countries. However the responsibility for Children's Services belongs to the Government of the country in which they are provided. This can be confusing, particularly where for instance a playworker works in two or more countries. Each of the four countries' children's services has children's welfare and best interests at the heart of all of their frameworks and policies. The following is a brief overview of some of these:

England

In England playworkers work within the framework of:

Every Child Matters (2004)

The Every Child Matters Green Paper developed from the Children Act 2004 outlined outcomes for children in five key areas:

1 Be healthy
2 Stay safe
3 Enjoy and achieve (play is included under this area. Playworkers advised to work to the Playwork Principles)
4 Make a positive contribution
5 Achieve economic well-being.

The 2004 Children Act put in place duties to ensure that local authorities support the fulfilment of these five outcomes. Although these may operate slightly differently from one local authority to another, they will all involve:

6 Creation of a local, secure, professionally maintained information child index (A database of all children accessing services in a local area with high levels of security. Supports communication between professionals and early identification of potentially vulnerable children)
7 Information sharing guidance
8 Multi-agency working guidance and multi-agency groups (Different agencies working with children co-operating. Can include such services as play and leisure, education, social services, voluntary and community sector, police, youth offending, health services etc.)
9 Use of a common assessment framework (CAF – this is a single assessment process which has to have the consent of parents, but can be instigated by any agency)
10 A Lead Professional (LADO – oversees investigations of allegations made against employees or volunteers that work with children)
11 Local Workforce Development Strategy for all people who work with children including playworkers. (To ensure that all have a common core of knowledge and skills including effective communication with children and families; knowledge of child development; supporting transitions; safeguarding and promoting the welfare of the child).

England now has a Children's Plan that includes planning for children's play provision. It also has a consultation on a play strategy 'Fair Play' that has grown out of The Children's Plan.

In 2008 the Government introduced into England a Statutory Framework – The Early Years Foundation Stage which sets out the legal requirements for learning, development and welfare for all children up to the 31 August following their fifth birthday. Play provision and playworkers who work with children in this age bracket are part of the regulatory system that requires them to be registered on an Early Years Register and inspected by OFSTED (Office for Standards in Education, Children's Services and Skills) to ensure their compliance with the regulations. Playwork provision and playworkers that work with children from the first September after their fifth birthday and up until the age of 8 have to be registered on the Childcare Register and although there is no duty of inspection 10% are randomly inspected by OFSTED to ensure there is compliance with the regulations that are relevant to them. Play provision and playworkers that work with children mainly over 8 may register on a Voluntary Childcare Register. Some play organizations thus fall into the bracket of being registered on all three registers.

The Independent Safeguarding Authority (ISA) is now operating the vetting and barring scheme related to recruitment and monitoring of playworkers and supercedes all previous systems. It is illegal to employ someone in regulated activity that has not been checked by ISA and who is not registered.

Reflection opportunity

The Early Years Foundation Stage has had (as with many change situations) its admirers and detractors. Are you regulated by the EYFS? Reflect on your experience of this and think about the positive and negative effects it has had on your work with children. If there are any negatives how can you turn these into positives? We are all subject to legislative changes in our lives and we have to ensure that we do not compromise our values but also work to the standards required by the government of the time.

At the time of writing there were some concerns related to registration with ISA. These ranged from concerns that it might deter or disincentivize appropriate individuals from seeking roles that involve working with children to potential for some people who had previously been registered having to pay again under the ISA system.

Wales

In Wales playworkers work within the The Children's and Young People's Plan (Wales) Regulations, 2007 which place a requirement on the Children and Young People's Partnership to prepare and publish a Children and Young People's Plan. The planning guidance for the plan is contained within the document 'Shared Planning for Better Outcomes'. The

Assembly Government has adopted the UN convention on the Rights of the Child as the basis for all its work for children and young people. This is expressed in 7 core aims to ensure that all children and young people:

1 Have developed a flying start in life and the best possible basis for their future growth and development
2 Have access to a comprehensive range of education, training and learning opportunities, including acquisition of essential personal and social skills
3 Enjoy the best possible physical and mental, social and emotional health, including freedom from abuse, victimization and exploitation
4 Have access to play, leisure, sporting and cultural activities (Wales is the only country in the United Kingdom to have a Play Policy (2002) and it also has a Play Strategy which is the plan for putting it into practice)
5 Children are listened to, treated with respect, and are able to have their race and cultural identity recognized
6 Have a safe home and a community that supports their physical and emotional well-being
7 Are not disadvantage by child poverty.

These aims form the basis for decisions on priorities and objectives nationally, and should also form the basis for decisions on strategy and service provision locally.

In Wales all playwork provision is regulated by a Welsh Statutory Instrument 'The Childminding and Day Care (Wales) Regulations' (2002) and Amendment (2003) which specify minimum standards for operation, children's welfare, registered persons etc. At the time of writing these regulations are due to be reviewed in the not too distant future.

Northern Ireland

In Northern Ireland playworkers work to:

Our Pledge (the ten-year strategy for children and young people in Northern Ireland (2006 – 2010))

The shared vision is for indicators that show that children and young people are:

1 healthy
2 enjoying, learning and achieving (Playboard Northern Ireland have a Play Manifesto – Giving Priority to Play)
3 living in safety and with stability
4 experiencing economic and environmental well-being
5 contributing positively to community and society
6 living in a society that respects their rights.

Playwork provision in Northern Ireland is regulated by the Children Order (1995) – Guidance and Regulations Volume 2, Family Support, Child Minding and Day Care, which sets the minimum standards of operation, suitability to work with children etc.

Scotland

Playwork provision in Scotland has to work to the National Care Standards revised (2005) that have as their main principles:

1 dignity
2 privacy
3 choice
4 safety
5 realizing potential (Playworkers in Scotland advised to work to the Playwork Principles and the Play Charter)
6 Equality and diversity

Scotland also has a separate system of registration for 'suitable persons'.

October 2004 saw the introduction of the first principles in Scotland for the Getting It Right for Every Child (GIRFEC). This is a national programme aimed at ensuring there is a co-ordinated approach across all agencies, which supports the delivery of appropriate and timely help to all children as they need it (Scottish Government). Ten core components are the foundation to the programme, which includes ensuring that children and young people are at the heart of any decisions. Protecting Children and Young People: The Charter was launched by Scottish Government in 2004. The Charter sets out what children and young people need and expect to help protect them when they are in danger of being, or already have been, harmed by another person. Developed by Save the Children in consultation and discussions with children and young people, it has proved to be user friendly and easily understood by children.

The Charter sets out what the child should expect from the adults such as minimize disruption to other parts of the child's life. Equally, there is a section in the Charter which gives the expectations of the child and their requirements from the adults, for example, listen to us, involve us, value us, get to know us. The Charter is published in posters and aimed at children. All playwork settings are expected by Care Commission – the Scottish Inspectorate to display a copy of the Children's Charter on the wall.

The Early Years Framework, which was launched in December 2008, aims to cover the interests and early interventions of children 0–8 years, using an integrated and multi-professional approach.

Reflection opportunity

What arrangements are there in your area for any of the above? Do you have contact with any other professionals in relation to any of the children you work with? If so what is your professional input? What particular knowledge do you have that may bring a useful perspective to the consideration of a child's needs or the fulfilment of any of the aims of the frameworks above?

The regulations that are mentioned above relate to various aspects of playwork and below we take a broad look at some of these.

Safeguarding children

The Oxford Dictionary defines 'safeguarding' thus:

1 to prevent something undesired
2 to guard or protect others' rights.

More recently safeguarding has been defined as:

1 'All agencies working with children, young people and their families taking all reasonable measures to ensure that the risks of harm to children's welfare are minimized; and
2 Where there are concerns about children and young people's welfare, all agencies taking appropriate actions to address those concerns, working to agreed local policies and procedures in full partnership with other local agencies' (Safeguarding Children, 2005)

Children, like all members of society have a right to a degree of protection from the hazards of life. Children also have the right to learn how to protect themselves and the same human rights as adults. Children of course should not be viewed solely as objects of concern, however they are, by nature of their immature development, and because of legislation (they are not allowed to be fully responsible for themselves until the age of 18) more vulnerable to exploitation, abuse and neglect than adults. Children are also more vulnerable to interference from outside agencies than adults and to having their rights usurped.

Safeguarding is a word that seems to incur an almost knee-jerk reaction in many people in the Children's Workforce, including playworkers. The reaction often seems to be 'stop – think – child protection'. Hopefully many people then get a second reaction that says 'no – wait – it's wider than that now . . . .' We say hopefully, because we do strongly hope that people working with children recognize the broader intentions of safeguarding that encompasses their rights to health and well-being as well as safety and security.

The trouble is that society has not only been obsessed with children and risk taking and ensuring that environments are virtually hazard-free (we explored this in Chapter 3); society has also been obsessed with protecting children from certain kinds of abuse.

There is a very real need for children to be protected from all kinds of things; predatory adults, exploitation, extreme danger, deliberate harm, domestic violence to name but a few. However, it seems that in our society many do not have a balanced view and in reality, in our efforts to keep children safe, we very often do the opposite and decrease their ability to keep themselves safe. We have also concentrated much of our efforts and money on certain issues, for example, child abuse (and sexual abuse in particular) in our attempt to make children safer.

This has had two main consequences. The first is that other issues where children also really need support, such as child poverty, teen pregnancy and parenting, access and addiction to alcohol and drugs, runaway children – all of which are supposedly on the increase do not engage us in the same way – we do not necessarily see children as victims in these situations and so we do not feel as angry or moved to respond.

The second consequence of society putting the spotlight on child abuse is that many of us are paranoid to a greater or lesser degree about the possibility of it happening. We have processes and procedures that often tie us playworkers up in knots trying to guarantee children's safety from possible or actual abusers. We imagine paedophiles round every corner. We worry about and sometimes report children playing doctors and nurses in the den. We try to have our eyes on our children wherever they go. Adults are either exhausted or in panic, children are no safer and their own views and feelings on all this are often ignored or have been influenced by adults.

Of course we are anxious for our children, but have we allowed that anxiety to be fuelled by the media and sidetrack us? The likelihood of being abducted and abused is less than the possibility of being hit by lightning. That does not mean however, that we insist on children wearing rubber boots at all times or going into underground bunkers during storms. The abduction of a child is of course a tragic event, but 'the press coverage and claim-making processes that follow such crimes can draw attention away from the more frequent and every day problems of children' (p. 226, Corsaro). Every week in this country, potentially dozens of children run away from abusive homes or die from drug abuse, but little of this finds its way into the newspapers or into our hearts and minds.

Key question

Returning to the dictionary definition above – what is undesired? What would we like to prevent happening to the children we work with and are we able in any way to do that?

You may find that the first things that come to mind include abuse, bullying and serious injury, as we have all been required to consider these. But did you also come up with any of the list below?

1 Bullying or being bullied
2 Serious or life-threatening injury
3 Serious or life-threatening illness
4 Abuse
5 Mental ill-health
6 Early pregnancy
7 Addiction

8 Boredom/limited positive experiences
9 Rejection
10 Underachievement
11 Bereavement

How many of these can we in playwork do something about in terms of prevention? We cannot ultimately stop any of these things happening to children outside of our setting, but we can still ensure that when they are in the play spaces we oversee, that they have access to a range of diverse experiences, support, information and observant, caring adults who do their utmost to listen to and empower them as well as respond to concerns following agreed procedures. This is also part of safeguarding.

It does include risk assessment of the environment. It does include having policies and procedures so that everyone knows what to do in the event of a fire, an accident, an emergency, a disclosure, etc. But it also means that we are aware of and advocate for children's rights, their needs, their responsibilities, that we have full regard for their personal identities, that we value who they are now and what they think and feel and that we care about the experiences they have.

In playwork this regularly means going the extra mile.

Reflection – Ali

I remember while doing some research a few years ago going to spend a day once with an organization who took children away on camp for a week. The organization had taken all the normal precautionary steps related to legal requirements. It was very laid-back with plenty of time and freedom for children to play how they wished, but at the same time there were opportunities available that were entirely new for these children, such as sleeping out under the stars, cooking on an open fire, experiencing the dawn chorus in the woods, mud-wrestling, looking after large farm animals, den-building with branches and pallets and sleeping in them if wanted . . . . Simple experiences – but the workers had thought deeply and worked hard to make them available because as one playworker said 'we want them to feel who they are and lay down some memories.'

So with specific regard to the above list of things that are undesired, playworkers should be aware of and up to date with the following issues.

Bullying

Remember that bullying is not everyday teasing and name-calling or even fighting (quite a lot of this is actually communication or rough and tumble play). Bullying is behaviour that is:

1 intentionally hurting another person
2 usually repetitive or persistent
3 uses physical and/or emotional aggression
4 involves an imbalance of power
   (Taken from www.anti-bullyingalliance.org.uk)

Playworkers should keep their eyes and ears open, take opportunities to listen and talk with children about bullying and talk with one another about any concerns they have in order to decide if any action should be taken (this may involve talking with parents or school or supporting individual children, passing on information on relevant websites, articles, etc.). We should also be aware of and honest about our own feelings and experiences of bullying as these can make us very subjective and negatively influence our interventions and conversations with children on this subject.

Injuries

Playworkers should:

1 have emergency first-aid skills or be able to refer to and support a first-aider colleague and know how to contact the emergency services
2 know the differences between accidental and non-accidental injuries
3 keep relevant records
4 ensure that risk assessments are done on particular activities, spaces or equipment.

Illnesses

Playworkers should:

1 know the signs and symptoms of childhood illnesses and know how to respond to these appropriately in relation to the specific child or children concerned and in order to protect the welfare of other children and workers at the setting
2 know how to support individual children with specific chronic illnesses in the event of an onset of symptoms or relapse.

Abuse

Playworkers should:

1 be aware of the indicators of different types of abuse
2 know what to do and who to contact if there is cause for concern
3 have information available from organizations like NSPCC or Kidscape
4 know what to do in the event of a disclosure
5 be aware of their own related reactions and responses
6 be able to discuss related issues with children when this is relevant.

Reflection opportunity

Here are some reflective scenarios related to child protection, children's rights, parental rights and the Playwork Principles. There are no right or wrong answers to these. Consider all possibilities and try not to jump to conclusions. ⇨

1 You become aware that a girl of 14, who comes to the after-school club as a junior helper, is regularly having consensual sex with her 17-year-old boyfriend. (You overhear her talking to a friend.) She is very playful, a great helper and the other children love her. How do you respond to this knowledge?

2 A 10-year-old boy, who you know comes from a very tough family and neighbourhood, has been coming to your adventure playground for over a year. He's formed a good relationship with all the playworkers and talks quite openly about his life. His dad's an alcoholic and unemployed and his mum's a recovering drug addict who is often depressed due to lack of money. She works intermittently as a cleaner. The boy obviously loves his mum and dad and you know often seems to be responsible for making meals for the family and generally looking after things. He is very capable and well organized and quite cheery. Do you consider it your duty to liaise with other professionals in relation to this boy and if so why and who?

Depression, mental illness

While the symptoms are hard to detect in childhood and tend to show up during adolescence, mental ill-health is on the increase in children. There is evidence to suggest that play deprivation is at least partly responsible; indeed Sturrock and Else propose that 'the maladapted play cycle (is) the kernel of neurosis' (p. 4, Colorado paper) and ask whether playworkers could 'enable the playing out of actual neurosis formation'. Certainly playworkers should be listening, watchful and reflective, providing as much diversity as possible over time in terms of space and materials for children to use as they wish.

Early pregnancy

Playworkers need to be aware of current facts and figures and know where to get advice and information locally on contraception and safe sex and to signpost young people to if the need arises. It will be helpful if they feel able to discuss these issues openly with children when relevant and debunk any myths they may have. However it is important to have policies that support this open form of communication so that parents know that the setting has information on these sorts of matters (see also below related to drugs). Playworkers will also be aware that children do often play with their emerging sexuality (usually well away from the eyes and ears of adults so that we don't know and can't stop it!). This is quite normal and we should only be concerned if we discover that there is a real age difference, one of the people concerned is not a child, there is a lack of consent or if it is happening while the children are in our care.

Addiction

Playworkers should be aware of the effects of different drugs and their local availability. They should have access to advice and information locally and get hold of good material that children and young people can also look at and/or take away to read. It's important to be able to talk about these issues without emotional baggage – having the respect of children and young people can go a long way down the prevention road.

The majority of children will at some point probably experiment – knowing the dangers will not necessarily prevent this – those who continue to seek out such experiences are often looking for escape from some present reality. The more that we can promote resilience in children (and this is a natural by-product of a wide range of freely chosen play experiences) the better.

Boredom

Some boredom is a good thing, because it can encourage new creative or imaginative thinking and action. A good playworker is always on the lookout for new (neophilic) stimuli – new 'junk', loose parts or materials to adapt or modify spaces, so that any of these can 'become available' at appropriate times.

Rejection, underachievement

We all experience these at different times in our lives and we cannot protect children from this, nor should we necessarily do so. Playworkers can however, build up emotional resilience through their respectful and positive relationships with children, through their provision of diverse play spaces and loose parts and through listening and 'being there' when needed.

Bereavement

Children may suffer loss in many ways. The intensity and frequency of their feelings and behaviour will vary depending upon the circumstance. Types of loss that may affect children:

> Bereavement; losing a pet; moving house or school; losing or leaving friends; parental separation; burglary; serious illness; failing to achieve; divorce.

Playworkers can help children make sense of loss in a number of ways:

1 Take your lead from the child and be prepared to talk about issues to do with loss and death and answer their questions honestly
2 Have books around that deal with these sensitive subjects
3 Be reassuring and comforting
4 Support children's expression of strong emotions and feelings
5 Provide opportunities for children to express their anger such as foam bats, clay, newspaper (for tearing and crumpling) etc. and physical activities such as digging and hammering to release angry energy and creative and make-believe resources such as free painting, puppets etc. for children to replay situations and feelings
6 Keep in contact with significant others such as parents and teachers
7 For major losses don't expect a quick resolution of the child's grief.

> ## Reflection opportunity
>
> 1 A child tells you that he doesn't like school and skips off sometimes and either goes to the local park to play, mainly on his bike or in the stream or goes to his granny's house. Do you share this information with anyone and if so why?
> 2 A child tells you that she has shoplifted at the local sweet shop with a group of friends. It was a laugh but now she feels guilty and isn't going to do it any more. Do you share this information with anyone else and if so why?
> 3 A child tells you that she's always fighting with her younger sister because she's so annoying and tries to use all her stuff. She also shows you the bruise that her sister made when giving her a 'Chinese burn'. Do you share this information with anyone else and if so why?

The second part of our definition of safeguarding was 'to guard or protect others' rights.' Which rights are these and how do we do this?

The United Nations Convention on the Rights of the Child

The United Kingdom signed up to this Convention and part of a playworker's role is to help defend children's rights wherever possible which are in summary as follows:

Civil and political rights – name and nationality; freedom of expression; freedom of thought, conscience and religion; meeting with others; protection of privacy; access to information; protection from abuse, neglect, torture or deprivation of liberty; right to be treated appropriate to age when caught breaking the law

Economic, social, cultural and protective rights – rights to life; decent standard of living; adequate provision for day-to-day care; high-quality health care; independence and inclusion for disabled children; a safe and healthy environment; education; rest, play and leisure activities; protection from exploitation; no involvement with armed conflict for under 15s.

What can we in playwork do to defend children's rights?

1 Ensure we have usable policies and procedures, related to safeguarding children, equality of opportunity, inclusion, health and safety, confidentiality and for providing for play and leisure activities, and use them
2 Listen to what children have to say; take it seriously and if and where necessary support them to find information and/or support relevant to their issues or concerns
3 Treat children as intelligent capable human beings
4 Get to know the children we work with and treat them with respect
5 Keep children's welfare uppermost in our thoughts and practices
6 Act as advocates for children and their play.

Health and safety

Health and safety are the responsibility of all adults who work with children. Playworkers must work within health and safety laws. Children, as other members of the public, have the right to an environment that will not cause them harm. Playworkers as all people who are employed, have the right to an environment that will not cause them harm. However, we do need to be sure that our understanding of health and safety requirements does not include us adhering to any of the myths that do the rounds periodically masking themselves as 'law'. One great example – that we are still coming across – is that egg boxes and/or toilet roll tubes must not be used because of the dangers of salmonella or gastroenteritis! Playworkers need to use their common sense and some critical thinking – check out what you are not sure about, rather than swallowing rumours and making assumptions. We equally need to be sure of what the requirements we should adhere to actually say. An example here would be the definition of supervision in the Daycare Standards often misinterpreted in practice by inspectors and playworkers alike, assuming that all children must be physically in the presence of playworkers at all times, whereas the guidance to the standards actually stated that supervision can be within sight or hearing (2001:27).

Risk and resilience

Children need to feel secure about their play settings and the playworkers who work in them. Parents need to know that their children are safe and in good hands. A safe and secure play environment however, is not one where all risk has been eliminated or where supervision is taken to mean never letting a child out of immediate sight! It is one where health and safety law is followed and all potential hazards are identified and risk assessed against their play-related benefits. Where the benefits for children outweigh the potential risks, the risks are managed. Interestingly a review commissioned by Bernardo's (2002) related to promoting resilience, discovered that 'Child welfare services have become more pre-occupied with risk factors than with factors which keep children healthy and safe'. Play is an important way that children learn about risk taking and gradually become resilient, by learning to cope with minor injuries, upsets and independent decision making. If all risk is eliminated from their lives, children do not learn how to be responsible for their own safety and they may be less able to recover from injuries and upsets later in life should these occur. Over-protection of a child is as dangerous as under-protection. (See section in Chapter 3 on Play and Risk Taking.)

In (2002:1–4) The Play Safety Forum issued a position statement in order to try to counteract the growing problem of play providers focusing on minimizing the risk of injury at the expense of other more fundamental objectives related to play and development. Insurance criteria and the fear of litigation seemed to be preventing many providers from offering a healthy range of play opportunities despite the fact that statistically playing in play provision is a comparatively low risk activity for children even when there are risky play opportunities on offer such as a zipline or a paddling pool. The position statement refers to

Photo 6.1 Will we make it?

'acceptable and unacceptable risk'. In determining, through risk assessment, 'acceptability', three things must be considered: The likelihood of coming to harm; the severity of that harm; the benefits, rewards or outcomes of the activity. Risk assessment then is an understanding of the balance between risks and benefits.

An important part of a playworker's role is to undertake and record formal risk assessments related to activities that are always likely to involve a certain amount of risk. For example using sharp tools or going pond dipping. (See below for examples of the risk assessment related to these.) Just as importantly playworkers must be able to assess risk ongoing, undertaking what we think of as dynamic risk assessment related to risks that unfold during play. For example children playing with a rope when the playworker notices that one child has tied it round the neck of another child pretending that he is a dog or children practising golf style swings with an umbrella and a small block of wood in a crowded play area. In these latter situations playworkers must assess the risks and make whatever intervention seems to best protect children from harm while enabling the benefits to still be achieved. For instance in the two cases mentioned it may be possible for the playworker to fashion a halter out of rope for the 'dog' and give a sponge to the golf players thus allowing the play to continue but without the risk of strangulation or injury.

It is also important, whenever possible to give children their own opportunity for assessing risk, as this is what they must eventually do in order to be responsible for their own safety.

Play England has recently published their implementation guide on risk management in play provision (2009) – this is a must-read for all playworkers as it adopts and promotes the risk-benefit analysis approach.

Reflection – Jacky

A colleague of mine gave a good example of this when a playscheme, she was quality assessing, went on a trip to a place called 'Slippery Stones'. This is a great natural place for play with a stream, pools and rocks (which may be slippery). The playworkers had done their risk assessment and, having visited the place themselves, one of the protective measures they had put in place was to ask children, who volunteered, to test out, under supervision, the slipperiness of the stones in the vicinity, the water depth of the pools and the state of the bottom of the pools to see if it was safe for children to jump/walk into the pools. The resultant fun was both risky yet controlled and the children had a wonderful time. Apparently one child had a minor scrape to the leg which was assessed by the First Aider.

Health and safety of the environment

An employer has a duty to ensure that the workplace is a healthy and safe place to work and each playworker has a duty to co-operate with this and to help keep themselves and others safe and healthy. Current Health and Safety Regulations (a poster or leaflets can be obtained from your local Health and Safety Executive) should be clearly displayed in all play settings in a place where they are easily viewed and their guidelines followed. All environments, equipment and materials should be checked regularly and in accordance with the settings Health and Safety Policy and used safely in line with any related instructions. Children should also be made aware of rules and regulations related to safety so that they too learn to see the importance of helping everyone to stay safe. Encourage children to report anything they consider to be dangerous. Children have the right to learn to protect themselves and others.

Reflection opportunity

Think about the Health and Safety Policy of your play provision. Reflect on whether it operates effectively. Are you satisfied with the arrangements? Are children given the chance to learn about things to do with their own health and safety? If not what can you do to try to help with this? Does the policy conflict with the Playwork Principles?

Contact your local Health and Safety Executive and Safeguarding Children Board and ask for free copies of any leaflets relevant to working with children. Can they advise you of any leaflets or posters that are designed for children to read?

Figure 6.1 Risk/Benefit assessment.

Play	Benefits	Hazards	Risks	Safety measures	Further action needed	Action carried out
Climbing trees	Physical development	Dead or weak branches	Falling – death or serious injury	Knowledge of children's individual abilities/approaches	Contact arboricultural expert	
	Confidence	Rough bark	Scratching	Restrictions in place		
	Risk assessment skills	Height from ground	Vertigo	Supervision by risk-aware and fit-to-climb playworkers		
	Sense of achievement	Awkward branches	Getting scared	Risk assessment gone through with children		
	Knowledge of nature	Fearless child	Getting stuck	Trees and ground under checked for suitability		
	Different view of environment		Going beyond ability	First Aider on hand		
	Test of own abilities					
	Freedom					
Using craft knives	Physical development (hand-eye co-ordination)	Sharp and pointed knife	Cutting or stabbing – death or injury to self	Safe storage and availability	None	
	Independence	Using incorrectly	Learn wrong use and damage things	Instruction on how and where to use safely		
	Fine motor skills	Holding incorrectly		Clear ongoing rules related to use		

				None
Confidence	Moving about while using	Cutting or stabbing others	Use of safety equipment	
Helps with creativity			Close supervision where needed by risk-aware playworkers	
Risk assessment skills			Regulated area for use of craft knives	
Concentration				
Karaoke				
Development of singing	Singing badly	Embarrassment	Knowledge of individual children's character	
Chance to show or develop ability	Not being able to sing	Ridicule	Playworkers who are prepared to make fools of themselves on occasion	
Fun	Moving awkwardly	Being laughed at	Safe atmosphere created	
Trying out adult culture	Drying up part way through		Distant supervision and intervention if necessary	
Confidence	Crying		Accompanying children who ask or show need for support	
Development of social skills				
Chance to be daft				

Reflection – Jacky

I remember a great play experience, one evening, at a junior club that I was involved with. Somebody had found a lot of old (out of date, but not dangerous, for those of you who are immediately concerned) first-aid stuff and asked a couple of the children if they wanted to help sort it out. It consisted of: first-aid boxes; first-aid instructions; different-shaped bandages; masks; safety pins; eye patches; plastic containers; gauze and cotton wool pads; tape etc. The club already had as part of its kit: an old stethoscope; a pair of crutches; a broken blood pressure machine; old blankets and some dressing up clothes that could be used for doctor or nurse uniforms. Within moments of discovering the wealth of potential the whole place was spontaneously transformed into a hospital and with the help of face (and ordinary) paints, children and playworkers were variously transformed into medical staff, the injured, dying and walking and non-walking wounded with terrible wounds and elaborate bandaging, slings etc. There were patients with every disease under the sun including some spectacular skin diseases and some truly horrifying mock operations being undertaken. It was a memorable evening and one which the children talked about for some time to come and often re-enacted bits of it, particularly the more gruesome 'operations'.

Trips out

Taking children off site is potentially fraught with organizational, health and safety, child protection and legal pot holes. However trips out are part of the stuff of childhood and thus it is well worth taking the time to plan well for both spontaneous and organized trips, so that they can be undertaken regularly.

If the children and you have decided on the trips you are going to undertake here are some important things to consider

1 Is there play value in the destination? Is it somewhere children might not otherwise go or have experiences they might not otherwise have?
2 Risk assessment – Do you have a risk assessment to cover the trip?
3 Written parental consent – Generic consent required for all basic, local and regular trips such as to the park and local shops; separate consent for longer and more distant trips such as to the seaside.
4 Information – Are your children well informed about all details of the trip such as: what to expect; what they can do; how long they will be out; particular behaviour required; safety issues etc.?
5 Insurance – Does your insurance cover off-site activities?
6 Travel –How will you get to where you are going? If using a vehicle does it comply with all legal requirements – is it roadworthy, insured, taxed, MOTed with seatbelts fitted to all seats? Sufficient seats for the numbers travelling? Fire extinguisher and First-Aid kit available? Minibuses require a permit as do their drivers. Is the driver licensed and over 21/25? If travelling by foot is there appropriate supervision, ratios and organization for the children to be safe? If travelling by public transport do you have an up-to-date timetable? Are the stops safe for the size of group you are taking etc.?
7 Children's records/contacts – Have you got all the information necessary to respond to children's individual needs, keep count of them and to make contact with carers in cases of delay, emergency etc.?
8 First Aid – A first-aid kit, accident book and someone with first-aid training required.
9 Contingencies – It is vital to have contingency plans for all potential problems, such as severe weather; accidents; delays; missing children; missing staff etc.

Reflection opportunity

Try to remember an enjoyable trip you went on as a child. What was it that made it so enjoyable? What part if any did the adults play in making the trip enjoyable? What part if any did the adults play in spoiling the trip? What should a playworker do on a trip in order to help keep the children safe, but at the same time help them enjoy themselves? Reflect on your own experiences as a child, but also as an adult, accompanying children on a trip.

Reflection – Jacky

I remember, as a 14-year-old, going on a youth club trip to a large country park, about an hour's bus ride from home, with three youth workers. I remember nothing about the trip other than that it prompted me and a few friends to go back to the same place a few weeks later. On this occasion we got soaking wet walking in watercress beds and we lost our way and ended up having to climb through some back gardens of some very large 'snooty' houses. I nearly got caught by a householder because my trousers snagged on a hook on a high wall we were climbing over and I only just escaped as the man shouted at me very angrily that he was going to call the police. I remember we ran through gardens and climbed walls at great speed until we got back onto a path that we recognized whereupon we all collapsed breathless and screaming with laughter about the escapade and our lucky escape. We were laughing all the way back home on the bus and endlessly repeated the tale, with actions, to each other and later to friends. The story and actions became more elaborate and daring with each telling. The householder became a maniac with a stick; I escaped being knocked unconscious by a fraction of an inch and a clever backward flip etc.

So what does this tell me, on reflection, about the role of adults on this trip? Had the youth workers not taken us on a trip to the park in the first place we may never have discovered it to go back to. So their role was one of introducing a new place. The angry householder added to the fun of risk taking and became a prop in an ever repeated narrative. He allowed me to become a bit of a hero in the eyes of my friends and his behaviour was a source of amusement to us, even though at the time I had been scared of getting caught and into trouble and of hurting myself trying to escape.

I remember accompanying a group of children on a trip to our local ice rink. I consider myself to be a good ice skater and so thought that I would spend much of the time helping children to be able to stay up and skate around on the ice. However this was not the case. I spent most of the time that we were there accompanying children backwards and forwards to the skate hire depot to change skates that were uncomfortable, had broken laces etc., or chatting to children who were tired and wanted to sit out and rest for a while. The children were mainly happy to do their own learning and practicing on the ice and supported each other's attempts. Adults not needed other than as a useful resource related to equipment or to pass a bit of time with when the children needed a rest.

Reflection – Ali

I remember a residential trip to the seaside – a decision was made to drive overnight as it was several hours away. We arrived just as dawn was breaking and we all got out to watch, on the cliff top. It was breathtaking and we couldn't speak. I've never forgotten it and have repeated it with other children since.

Equality of opportunity

Equal opportunities law comes into various aspects of playwork such as employment, staffing and provision for disabled children. However equality of opportunity is not just about following the law, it is also about good playwork practice, working within the Playwork Principles and following a moral and ethical approach.

> 'Respect comes when you know your friend is not exactly like you but you still like her in spite of and because of those differences'. (1994:225)

Play is a cultural phenomenon. It is 'a dominant activity of children in all cultures (and), is viewed to be both cause and effect of culture' (1994:5). We live in a diverse world with many cultures being represented within our society. Indeed each play provision should represent a microcosm of its potential local user group. In order to give all local children knowledge that the play setting is for them, it is vital that it represents the many cultures that are part of the local neighbourhood and that it also supports cross-fertilization of those many cultures in order that the culture of the provision is uniquely and directly influenced by and reflects all of the children who attend – the greater the diversity the richer the provision.

Play is a right for all children as enshrined in Article 31 of the UN Convention on the Rights of the Child (1995:6). 'Enabling all children to play, and to play together, is about a benefit to the whole community. It is not about overcoming legal hurdles or making expensive provision for a small section of the community. If any child is prevented from playing then it diminishes the play experience of all' (2007:1). Although this is a quote related solely to including disabled children into mainstream provision for play, it really relates to any child with regard to their: social and financial status, gender, race, colour, ethnic or national origin, belief, religion, family status, nationality, lawful sexual preference, ability, health (physical or mental) and age (hereinafter known as 'all children'). It also relates to all types of provision staffed by all types of playworkers.

If we 'enable' participation of all children to happen, we make a conscious decision and take practical action to ensure that participation of all can happen. This is not the same as 'wanting' participation of all to happen, or hoping that participation of all happens. 'To enable' is an active verb; it requires ongoing action related to inclusion of all including monitoring and evaluation. By this continuous action cycle we ensure two things – that nobody is prevented from participating if they wish to participate but that also the provision is geared to the widest range of children possible thereby positively attracting participation of all.

Equality and inclusion of all

We have a legal duty not to discriminate on the grounds of race, gender or disability, but sometimes we unknowingly prevent some children from participating in our play provision.

Photo 6.2 Girls climb too.

Equality means recognizing and enjoying difference and ensuring that each child and adult is treated with equal respect and has equal access to what the provision has to offer.

What actions should we take to ensure that all children have the potential to be included in play provision and have equality of play opportunity when they do attend?

The KIDSactive Playwork Inclusion Project (PIP) produced a useful checklist called 'All of Us' (undated) and the following is an adaptation of its key features.

1 The attitudes and behaviour of the playworkers and children demonstrate how unremarkable it is that children of all statuses, genders, races, ethnicity, abilities, health, beliefs, religions, nationalities, sexuality etc. are part of a wide cross-section of the local community using the service.

2 Play opportunities are led by the interests and enthusiasms of each child who attends and take place with regard to any likes, dislikes and specific needs each child may have.

3 Everyone is welcomed on arrival and wished well on departure in a way that suits them.

4 Pictures, equipment and resources reflect the lives of people from all cultures, categories and walks of life as part of a wide representation of children's differing backgrounds and experience.

5 The person in charge is committed to the active participation of children, workers, (parents and others where appropriate) to ensure good-quality provision and to ensure that individual needs are met.

6 The person in charge has made time to build links with families, local services, schools, community groups etc. as part of a commitment to give all local children and families a genuine choice to be part of the service.

7 All playworkers have had attitudinal training around a range of equality issues and continue to take part in training about inclusion.

8 All playworkers are aware that attitudes, environments, structures and policies need ongoing attention in order that they do not disadvantage particular children.

9 All playworkers have or are developing skills to communicate effectively with each child, and encourage all children to develop ways of communicating with each other.

10 Each child has opportunity to express their views and opinions on the play provision and the sessions they attend, using whatever communication methods they choose.

11 Parents and carers feel welcome and valued when they offer information that helps the play provision enable their child to take a full part.

12 The service has a vision of what it wants to do; policies and procedures for how it does it; and a process of monitoring and evaluation to see how well it is doing it. This includes all who are involved in the setting in a process of continuing reflection on the development of inclusive policy and practice.

Prejudice

At times, some children, as with some adults, are prey to their prejudices and this may make them behave in a discriminatory way. Playworkers have to make decisions about when and how they intervene in the play process and this includes situations where prejudice is apparent. It is standard practice in most childcare provision to intervene and challenge all discriminatory language and behaviour as soon as it happens in a calm, informative non-inflammatory manner in order that the adult, child or children realize that you find their behaviour unacceptable; learn why it is unacceptable; change their behaviour in the future and to support the child, children or adult who are being discriminated against. However it is important to reflect on discriminatory situations before you intervene in the same way as you do in other situations in order to ensure that you are not by default imposing an adult-led agenda on the child or children rather than giving them the opportunity to sort the matter out for themselves and in their own way. Clearly, if you find behaviour or language offensive it is important to let them know that you disapprove, however that may be sufficient.

Reflection – Jacky

This happened in a local park when I was with my young grandchildren. It was not a playwork situation, but could easily have been.

When we arrived at the fixed play area there was a group of seven children already there – four black girls of about 11 years of age and three white boys of a similar age, with another slightly younger boy hanging about. The three boys were up the top of a climbing frame all looking down at the black girls who were giggling and talking together in a foreign language but to the boys in unbroken English. The boys were taunting the girls in what seemed to be a very unpleasant racist way which was also peppered with swearing, saying such things as 'you f****** lot need us to come to your country and provide you with medicine because you are all dying of aids' and 'You should only talk in English when you're in England. It's rude to gabble in that sh**** African way'. I was appalled and thought I'm going to have to say something. Then the girls retaliated saying such things as 'You whiteys are so lazy we have to come to your country in order to do the jobs that none of you want to do including workings as doctors and nurses' and 'you English are just as dull as your weather and you're all stupid. You've got nothing sensible to say.' and 'you lot are all flabby and pale and boring'. The boys took it in turns to try their hands at insults and the girls laughed and waved their hands around excitedly as they jeered at the boys and ridiculed them for their pathetic attempts. The girls definitely had the upper hand. Watching the group as they hurled insults at each other it became apparent that this was a form of young 'flirting', which although unpleasant in its prejudice can be seen replicated in all manner of ways with groups of pre-pubescent boys and girls. After overtly looking at the group for a while and a little reflection I decided that on behalf of my two young grandchildren I should show that I didn't like what they were saying so I said to the group 'Do you mind' and I said to my three-year-old grandson 'They're being really silly aren't they'.

Key question

If this had been a playwork situation consider what you would have done and why? What sorts of play were being represented in the scenario above?

As playworkers we must use good play centred methods and have good play centred reasons for intervening in situations when our intervention may prevent children from following their own instincts and ideas, in their own way and for their own reasons. Playwork is not a profession that has modification of children's behaviour as one of its aims. It has at its heart the belief that children learn and develop specific aspects of themselves during their free, non-adult directed play and that an excess of adult intervention will prevent this learning and development from happening. This also includes learning and development that happens in some unpleasant situations as well as in pleasant ones.

Discrimination

When we discriminate we recognize difference. Knowledge of difference can be used in a positive way to better support equality of opportunity and fairness, or it can be used in a negative way to support prejudice and/or unfair treatment of children and adults on the grounds of their difference.

There are two types of negative discrimination:

Direct discrimination – this is when one person is treated less favourably than another in the same or similar circumstances.
Indirect discrimination – this happens when a policy is applied equally to everybody but has the result of excluding a particular person or people.

Here are examples of the two forms of discrimination in action:

Direct discrimination

Two children, one of whom is in a wheelchair have been verbally abusing a black girl using racist taunts, over a period of time. Both have previously been given verbal warnings for their behaviour. They are caught again. The able-bodied child is excluded from the provision for 2 days and the disabled child is given another verbal warning on the grounds that she is being 'led on' by the other!

Reflection opportunity

Think about this last example. Who is being discriminated against and in what ways? How might you respond in all the circumstances described?

Reflection – Jacky

I remember (with some adult shame) occasionally playing with two boys who lived across the road from me when I was about eight years old. We would play at cowboys and Indians (as it was then called) and I was instructed on how to play. One of the boys, Phillip was the son of a wealthy family and the other was their foster son. In our games the foster son was always captured and tied to a tree outside their house while Phillip and I ran off 'victorious' that we had defeated 'the baddy'! I suspect, sadly looking back on the whole thing that the foster son was never treated as an equal and had been fostered to provide a play mate for Phillip, who was an overbearing, but neglected, boy. If this happened at a play provision staffed by playworkers and someone intervened would this be adulteration or an acceptable intervention?

Indirect discrimination

Children at the provision all choose with whom they wish to sit on a coach trip to the seaside except for two who are forced to sit together because nobody else will sit with them. One is new to the setting, is shy and has no real friends yet and the other has learning difficulties and the child she initially chose to sit next to wanted to sit with somebody else.

Reflection opportunity

Think about this last example. Is this indirect discrimination and if it is, who is responsible for it occurring? How could this situation have been avoided without taking away some element of choice from the children? Should children be given free choice in all situations?

Reflection – Jacky

Many years ago I worked as a part-qualified assistant youth worker in a youth club in an area that was predominately Asian. The youth club was very popular with white young people but only two young Asian men, and no young Asian women, attended. The youth club was also totally off limits to the gypsies who lived in the area. At the time I did not understand why this was happening. After later Equal Opportunities training, undertaken as part of my other occupation as a lecturer in further education, I realized that indirect discrimination had been happening. There was nothing on offer that would be attractive or acceptable to young people of either gender from the Asian community and because the gypsy children were not on the Electoral Register they could be excluded! Later when I became involved in playwork I reflected on my own ignorance and that of the people in charge of youth work in the area in relation to providing for all young people. Happily most playworkers today are far better informed in relation to inclusion of all children.

In this chapter we have tried to put a reflective playwork slant on some of the legal aspects of working with children that have relevance to playworkers. There may be other areas that you consider to be important. Try to reflect on these with the Principles of Playwork in mind. Do these Principles impact on or inform the way that you implement these things?

Useful contacts

www.childline.org.uk – charitable organization offering information and help lines to children and young people needing help or advice

www.childrenslegalcentre.org.uk – an independent national charity concerned with law and policy affecting children and young people.

www.crin.org.uk – the Child Rights information network – committed to all aspects of children's rights, legal and otherwise.

www.hse.gov.uk – the Health and Safety Executive provides information about everything to do with health and safety

www.kids-online.org.uk – campaigning organization offering training and up-to-date information/publications regarding the rights of disabled children and inclusive play services

www.playengland.org.uk – for a free copy of the Managing Risk in Play Provision: Implementation Guide

www.playwork.org.uk – the National Playwork Unit at Skillsactive supports playwork education and training and playworkers in a range of ways. It provides links to interesting websites on the links page.

www.rospa.com – The Royal Society for the Prevention of Accidents promotes safety related to all areas of life including play

www.standards.dfes.gov.uk – information about the Early Years Foundation Stage

References

Davy, A. and Gallagher, J. (2006) *New Playwork: Play and Care for Children 4–16.* Fourth Edition. London: Thomson Learning.

Department for Education and Skills (2003) *Out of School Care: National Standards for Under 8s Day Care and Child-minding.* Nottingham DfES Publications.

Department for Education and Skills (2007) *Practice Guidance for the Early Years Foundation Stage.* Nottingham DfES Publications.

Department for Education and Skills (2007) *Statutory Framework for the Early Years Foundation Stage.* Nottingham DfES Publications.

Department of Health COS©CNI (2003) *What to Do if You are Worried a Child is Being Abused.* Department of Health. London. Department of Health Publications.

John and Wheway (2004) quote taken from 'Can Play, Will Play: Disabled Children and Access to Outdoor Playgrounds'. London: National Playing Fields Association in Play Wales (2007) *Inclusive Play and Disability.*

KIDSactive Playwork Inclusion Project (PIP) (undated) *All of Us – The Framework for Quality Inclusion* Kids, DFES, Sure Start.

Lasater, C. and Johnson, J. E. (1994) Culture, Play and Early Childhood Education in *Children's Play in Diverse Cultures.* Roopnarine, J. Johnson, J. and Hooper F. (Eds). Albany: State University of New York Press.

Maclean, I. and Maclean, S. (2006) *From Birth to Eighteen Years: Children and the Law.* Kirwin Maclean Associates. Rugely. Kirwin Maclean Associates.

Newman, T. (2002) *Promoting Resilience: A Review of Effective Strategies for Child Care Services – Summary.* Centre for Evidence Based Social Services. University of Exeter http://www.barnardo's.org.uk/resources

Shier, H. (1995) *Article 31 Action Pack Children's Rights and Children's Play.* Birmingham: Play-Train.

West Yorkshire Learning Provider Equality Network (2004) '*Equality and Diversity – What's That Then?*' Bradford: Learning and Skills Council.

Quality in Playwork 7

This chapter will look at different quality systems and standards that have related to playwork in a variety of ways and will consider how these systems have impacted on the quality of play provision – or not, as the case may be. We will also look at how playwork is managed and some of the management issues that are specific to and in playwork.

What do we mean by quality?

Quality has become a popular word in recent years. Like many over-used words, it can cease to have real or inspirational meaning in practice. Essentially it means 'possessing a high degree of excellence' or 'the standard of how good something is when measured against other similar things'. So it is essential that any standards used to measure the quality of playwork practice are relevant to playwork and enable self-assessment or an 'inspector' to measure the quality of actual playwork practice, not some other form of practice. Such assessment is also a comparative measure that has to be able to compare one provision to another provision that works within the same ethical framework and has similar aims. Herein lies a major problem because although playwork does have a similar ethical framework as other professions working with children, and it deals with some of the same issues such as protecting and caring for children, it certainly does not have the same aims as education, childcare or youth work. Many of the standards that have been used to measure the quality of playwork provision are not relevant to playwork and this is something that most politicians, inspectors, educators, early years workers, youth workers and many parents and members of the general public have not understood. (See Chapter 8.)

Playwork is play and child focused. Many quality systems are very adult focused, measuring standards based on adult-orientated outcomes or ideas. So let us reflect back to our own 'quality measures' that we used when we were children. What made something a good play experience? How aware were we of what we wanted? What made something a good resource or another child or adult a good playmate?

Reflection opportunity

Think back to either one or several good play experiences that you had when you were a child – from when you were both fairly young and older. Can you remember what it was on these occasions that made the play experience a good one? What made you look forward to something? Thinking now as an adult, would you use the same measures to assess whether it was a good play experience? If not, what standards would you apply to see whether the experience was a 'good' one? Could you apply either your child or grown-up measure to children's play experiences happening now?

We can probably all relate to occasions when – as parents or playworkers – we have seen children having what looks like the time of their lives at some new place or doing some new thing and then asking them afterwards whether they had had a good time, only to hear them say 'it was alright' or 'I didn't like that big kid' or 'I liked those sweets'. Being 'in the moment' is something that many children are unable to verbalize outside of that 'moment' if indeed at all and this leads to a problem of children's perception in relation to their own play. However, do we as adults have a right to think that we know what a 'quality measure' is in relation to play?

So if playwork is play and child focused, whose standards should we be using to measure playwork practice? If it is those set by children, this leads to yet another problem. Although there is currently a huge emphasis on including children in any number of decision-making processes, a lot of people in the playwork sector would suggest that many of the techniques used to consult children, actually interfere with their play process; are heavily weighted to ensure that the 'right' answers are achieved; are an irrelevance; are unlikely to come up with any results that truly reflect what children think and so forth.

Reflection – Jacky

I have seen the results of a survey carried out with children where the results showed that children valued 'conservation' in their play as well as 'equality of opportunity' and other very adult notions that surely are not a true reflection of what the majority of children value about playing. Children can be easily manipulated!

Surely it is only by reflective practice – reflectively watching how children use a play environment and the resources within it; unobtrusively listening to what children say when they are

Photo 7.1 New view of the world.

playing; actively listening in a non-judgemental way when children are talking to you; reflecting back on your own and other's play experiences and reading the literature – that we can find out what children need for their playing and then go on to decide whether our playwork supports that.

Recent quality standards

Let us turn to look at what has been in use to decide on the quality of playwork provision to date. In the last few years there have been four main types of standards or measures applied to playwork provision as follows:

Out of school care standards

These statutory standards stemmed originally from the Care Standards Act 2000 and were a set of outcomes that providers aimed to achieve. Included within them were regulations that had to be met that originated from the Children Act 1989. As from September 2008 these no longer applied in England, but they were the quality standard for the previous decade. Playwork settings working with younger children (under 8 years old) had to register and were inspected against the following standards, the substance of which is still contained within the new standards in England that are part of the Early Years Foundation Stage. (See Chapter 6.)

Standard 1 – Suitable person
Checking that the person/people in charge and all other staff are vetted, monitored and suitable to work with children.

Standard 2 – Organization
Checking on the practical organization of staff, children, space and resources.

Standard 3 – Care, learning and play
Checking that plans and observations for this are regularly undertaken.

Standard 4 – Physical environment
Checking that this is warm, welcoming, adequate, clean and safe both indoors and out.

Standard 5 – Equipment
Checking that equipment and materials are stimulating, safe and positive.

Standard 6 – Safety
Checking that all health and safety regulations and procedures are adhered to.

Standard 7 – Health
Checking on practice and procedures for health and hygiene.

Standard 8 – Food and drink
Checking that this is healthy, nutritious and caters for individual needs.

Standard 9 – Equal opportunities
Checking that the diverse needs of individual children are understood, valued and met.

Standard 10 – Special needs
Checking that disabled children and children with additional needs are valued and included.

Standard 11 – Behaviour
Checking on implementation and review of policies and strategies for responding to behaviour.

Standard 12 – Working in partnership with parents and carers
Checking on how a setting relates to, involves and informs parents and carers.

Standard 13 – Child protection

Checking that knowledge, understanding of and procedures related to child protection are in place and being used.

Standard 14 – Documentation

Checking that all necessary documents, records, policies and procedures are kept and securely stored.

Open access provision had various alterations to the detail in the criteria in order to cater for the different circumstances in which they operate, but were nevertheless expected to comply with much that was contained within the standards.

Reflection – Jacky

I have witnessed some very contorted efforts on the part of playscheme workers to get information back from parents so that they had emergency contact numbers etc. that relate to health and safety and child protection procedures, in case of a child having an accident. On one particular occasion this involved a child being given a form to take home to his parents asking for personal information; followed by a parent storming down to the playscheme to ask 'What the **** do you want this information for?'; followed by a partial completion of the form that did not seem to include the required information and the playworkers deciding that it would have to be a 'good enough' compliance with the regulations!

Early years foundation stage

These above standards have now been replaced in England by the standards written into the Early Years Foundation Stage, which are similar and altogether in summary cover the following which are variously applied depending upon the registration of the organization (see Chapter 6).

Welfare requirements

1 Safeguarding and promoting children's welfare
2 Suitability of persons
3 Suitability of premises, environment and equipment
4 Organization
5 Documentation

Learning and development requirements

1 Early learning goals
2 Educational programmes
3 Assessment of achievement

Areas of learning and development

1 Personal, social and emotional
2 Communication, language and literacy
3 Problem solving, reasoning and numeracy
4 Knowledge and understanding of the world
5 Physical development
6 Creative development

Since devolution in the United Kingdom and particularly in the last couple of years, standards and inspectorates have all been changing and each country now operates slightly differently and is informed by newer and different legislation. England is inspected by Ofsted (Office for Standards in Education, Children's Services and Skills), Wales by the CSSIW (Care and Social Services Inspectorate Wales), Scotland by the SSSC (Scottish Social Services Council) and Northern Ireland by Social Services Inspectors from Early Years Teams, currently moving from the Department of Health, Social Services and Public Safety to the Department of Education.

On the whole, the playwork sector has had a lot of difficulty with these standards, because they were written to cater for childcare provision. Playwork ended up being regarded as synonymous with childcare ever since the UK Government introduced the Childcare Strategy in 1998 with masses of funding to set up before and after-school clubs and holiday clubs so that parents could work. The differences between being a playworker and being a group childminder have been misinterpreted and debated ever since – and one of the real problems has been that most inspectors were familiar with early years childcare and applied the same thinking to out of school play provision.

This has caused and continues to cause significant problems with many clubs and play-schemes doing good playwork being judged as only adequate or less, because the standards were not written to judge playwork and the majority of inspectors had no playwork experience themselves. In many instances, the standards have been perceived – and sometimes used – as a whip to judge and chastise, rather than as a tool to measure whether practice was good enough and how to improve it. Lots of other settings have ended up doing no playwork and purely offering care and education (but very often still being called playworkers which compounds the problem further). While a number of inspectors have been open and flexible and there have been some great success stories here and there of good relationships and under-standing between inspectors and settings, these have sadly been in the minority and playwork continues to struggle with its externally applied childcare label and the perceptions of what this means.

Examples we have come across over the years include inspectors:

- insisting that a setting does not allow any child to access its outdoor areas because a gate was found unlocked at the time of the inspection – this took over six months to resolve and so throughout the summer children were kept indoors;
- telling a setting that no under-8's can use scissors

- maintaining that a setting must take the refrigerator temperature three times a day
- requiring that a setting stop using cardboard boxes for play because (a) they have sharp edges and (b) they are a fire risk.

To be fair, these are extreme examples. Ali has run training with many inspectors and the majority were conscientious people trying to interpret the standards correctly. The biggest sticking points were usually over planning (playworkers plan for child-led space and resources rather than decide on every-day developmental activities) and safety (playworkers afford children opportunities for risk taking in play) because both of these issues are interpreted so differently when working with much younger children and most inspectors come from a childcare background. Many less experienced or savvy playworkers have seen their inspector as the mouthpiece of some deity and taken what they say as the gospel truth not to be questioned – we have spent much time on training courses convincing playworkers that they can talk to and challenge their inspectors. However, we have also come across and/or supported many playworkers who have entered into dialogue with their inspectors and explained and surmounted these differences and won Ofsted acclaim.

Reflection opportunity

What has been your experience or involvement with these standards and their inspection? Have you been able to constructively challenge inspectors where this has been needed – or supported others to do so?

National occupational standards

National occupational standards (NOS) establish the benchmark of competence required in a sector, and playwork has its own NOS at levels 2, 3 and 4. These have been and continue to be written and reviewed/revised by a SkillsActive committee made up of playworkers, playwork employers, playwork trainers, assessors and verifiers, and consulted on in the field. These standards describe in groups of units and elements, the job function of a playworker at entry level through to management level and they are used in a number of ways:

a as assessment criteria for an S/NVQ in playwork
b as the basis for learning outcomes of syllabi in vocational qualifications in playwork
c to inform job descriptions and person specifications
d to inform quality assurance schemes
e for staff training needs analysis and appraisal.

The positive outcomes of these standards include

1 improvement in practice
2 more widespread recognition of playwork as a profession

3 creation of a range of playwork-specific qualifications
4 far greater understanding among playworkers of playwork theory
5 more coherence and agreement within the playwork sector itself
6 informing ongoing professional development.

The less positive effects of the standards include

1 poor assessment by non-occupationally competent assessors and verifiers
2 misinterpretation and misunderstanding of wording
3 slavish compliance with the minutiae
4 not using the standards as a basis for learning, reflection and an improvement of current practice
5 less flexibility, spontaneity and imagination on the ground – perhaps a loss of playful spirit
6 standards only apply to individual rather than organizational competence.

Reflection opportunity

What has been your indirect involvement or direct experience with Playwork NOS or with their assessment? Can you add to the positive effects above? Were you able to do anything about any ineffective consequences that occurred?

We have both been external verifiers for the Playwork NVQ and visited many assessment centres and seen both good and bad assessment and/or playwork practice. We have seen centres where assessors are passionate about play and playwork and about their candidates, who clearly have improved their understanding and delivery of playwork during their assessment process. Equally so, we have seen others who are constrained by funding, give little support to candidates, insist on lots of written evidence and worst of all, care little about good playwork. We always supported and encouraged development in centres who wanted to improve and we did see many centres really enhance their practice, but we also did have to take steps to prevent some centres from even offering the NVQ.

Reflection – Jacky

I have seen some real leaps in depth of understanding when a few level 3 playwork candidates have gone on to undertake level 4 NVQ in playwork. This has required them to research play theories as well as other aspects of playwork in some depth and has resulted in some very deeply analytical reflective practice which in turn brought about some truly excellent play provision.

Best Play objectives

'Best Play – what play provision should do for children' was published in 2000 as a result of a partnership between the National Playing Fields Association, PLAYLINK and the Children's

Play Council. It was quite a ground-breaking document in that it set out to clarify and give acknowledgement to the playwork profession and its values, through identifying and recognizing the benefits ('outcomes') that children can receive from attending 'best' playwork provision. The authors were at pains to point out that it was written as guidance and 'is neither a quality assurance scheme nor a set of standards' (p. 19) but it does to go on to say that the seven simple play objectives (see below), could form the basis for such evaluation, because they state what play provision aims to do for children. The document goes on to list indicators and possible evaluation methods for each objective.

1. The provision extends the choice and control, which children have over their play, the freedom they enjoy and the satisfaction they gain from it.
2. The provision recognizes the child's need to test boundaries and responds positively to that need.
3. The provision manages the balance between the need to offer risk and the need to keep children safe from harm.
4. The provision maximizes the range of play opportunities.
5. The provision fosters independence and self-esteem.
6. The provision fosters children's respect for others and offers opportunities for social interaction.
7. The provision fosters the child's well-being, healthy growth and development, knowledge and understanding, creativity and capacity to learn.

Best Play was the first evaluative tool for playwork provision that was playwork-specific, had a wide readership and was well received. However, it probably achieved more in educating the wider workforce – which was welcomed and very necessary – than it did in getting workers on the ground to regularly evaluate their day-to-day practice.

We have both known several after-school clubs and playcentres that have successfully used the 7 Best Play objectives as the basis for their Play Policy. The objectives gave them a useful platform to explain some of their playwork practices, as it is couched in language, and uses outcomes, that are considered acceptable, even desirable, by most people, both inside and outside the playwork field, while still retaining some of the less acceptable and easily understandable aspects of playwork such as; children having personal control; children testing boundaries; and offering opportunities for risk taking.

Quality assurance schemes

'A quality assurance system is a structured approach to identifying the standards that you aim to meet and a systematic way of monitoring all areas of work to ensure that you are meeting or working towards those standards' (p. 10. QiP).

There have been a number of schemes in recent years, both national and local, that settings have used voluntarily or been encouraged to use by inspectors or employers and there are new ones presently being created. Some have been developed by national organizations like the National Childminding Association and the Preschool Learning Alliance or by local authorities or childcare partnerships, but these have all been childcare based and aimed at very young children.

The main ones that have been used in playwork settings and have been endorsed by the Government's quality assurance framework 'Investors in Children', have been Aiming High (developed by 4Children, formerly Kids Clubs Network) and Quality in Play (developed by London Play). Aiming High has been used the most as it was more widely known, but in fact it is only Quality in Play that is playwork-specific.

Undertaking a quality assurance scheme programme is a bit like doing a slightly simpler national vocational qualification, except it is the organization that is judged as opposed to the individual. The organization has to identify its good practice and then put together a portfolio of evidence to show they meet the scheme's criteria. A scheme-appointed assessor will visit and judge the organization accordingly.

Quality in Play is now administrated and overseen by Play England but Wales and Northern Ireland have liaised with the scheme developers in the process of generating similar schemes themselves and the programme criteria are also being updated.

Quality in Play is definitely directly relevant to playwork but even then, in our experience, we would say that using the scheme to really measure and inspire good practice, will depend on:

1 whether settings themselves choose to do it
2 whether scheme mentors and assessors are occupationally competent, knowledgeable and passionate about playwork
3 whether managers impose the scheme on settings without offering personalized support.

Reflection opportunity

Have you been involved with a quality assurance scheme? Was it playwork-specific? Did it result in freer play and a richer play environment? Was the process reflective (if so, it should promote change)?

The First Claim

The First Claim was published through Play Wales in 2001 but has been widely acclaimed and used across the United Kingdom. It described itself as 'a framework for playwork quality assessment' and is essentially a graded self-assessment tool for playworkers at basic and intermediate levels. The advanced level is depicted in a second publication entitled *The First Claim – Desirable Processes* (2003). These frameworks promote and encourage ongoing personal reflective practice on how a playworker:

1 creates and resources play environments
2 recognizes the intervention styles they use

3 observes and recognizes children's moods and play behaviours
4 observes and recognizes play types
5 recognizes their own modes of intervention at different times
6 observes and recognizes children's play mechanisms.

Although it was written primarily for self-assessment and to encourage a much deeper awareness of one's own practice, elements of it can be and have been used to promote improved
practice within playwork teams and as the basis for supervision sessions.

It has however, been mostly used as reading material – this has been a very positive
educative tool and many people have benefited from this – but the benefits to children would
be much greater if it was related to practice and used according to its original intention! It
continues to be absolutely relevant to playwork practice, but it also does need updating and
Play Wales are intending to do this.

Key question

Have you read both publications? Have you used them as a means of reflective practice?

Reflection – Ali

I have personally used First Claim in a number of ways. I have applied the advanced framework to my own
practice in a residential summer playscheme – I found it both fascinating and incredibly useful. It helped me
identify more clearly both my 'playwork persona', that is, the way I am around children at different times and
in various circumstances, and the particular fears I have that can cause me to unnecessarily intervene or
misinterpret playing behaviours. In conjunction with colleagues we have also used them as a framework to
'assess' each other over a period of time and feed back our findings to each other in a group discussion. That
required a lot of trust but the insights we gained were really worthwhile.

Reflection – Jacky

I have helped some playwork supervisor/managers to successfully use First Claim as part of their Supervision
and Appraisal Scheme. This has led to far greater reflection on the play focused aspects of playwork practice
at the setting.

So to summarize this excursion into quality assurance – How do we know outstanding
playwork when we see it – what makes it not just exemplary but exceptional? In order to
decide on the quality of playwork provision, clear standards or criteria are obviously needed
in order to make judgements. But there are still issues here; namely, who sets the standards;
who uses them for assessment purposes; and how are they used? Even when the standards are

good and the assessors are good, playwork practitioners can end up using the standards in a way that tries to 'conform to procedures' rather than genuinely reflecting on their work. Thus conformity takes the place of reflection and there is nothing in any Quality Assurance System or Playwork Principle that suggests that 'conforming' is a part of playwork!

We have seen that a number of criteria and standards have been in place and used to measure playwork. Only a few are directly relevant to playwork – here again the playwork sector has its work cut out in getting this message out more widely. We have also seen that even for those standards that are playwork-specific to work well and genuinely measure and improve practice, they must be administered properly, used by people occupationally competent in playwork and undertaken in a reflective spirit that truly wishes to know how to enhance and advance playwork practice.

When all is said and done, our sector's quality marker must be the Playwork Principles, because these establish the professional and ethical framework for playwork. In a first-class setting, these principles would *always* underpin what the playworkers do, for example, they will always intervene in a way that will extend play, or they will always act as advocates for play in the face of adult agendas and so on. All standards and criteria to judge playwork must be wholly steeped in the Principles – if they are not, they are not just irrelevant, they may well distort and damage practice.

Reflection opportunity

Do the Playwork Principles genuinely underpin your playwork practice or the practice in settings you know? If not, how could they?

Of course, ensuring quality playwork provision should be the responsibility of managers – they are the people who oversee delivery of the whole. Are managers themselves properly equipped for this and what does that mean? Let's look at the business of management a bit more closely.

Management issues

Who are the managers in playwork? They may be a management committee made up of either a hotchpotch of local people (anyone prepared to take on the role) or perhaps school staff and or local community people; the governors of a school; the owner of an out of school club; a local authority senior, middle or junior manager in a department such as Leisure or Social Services that is responsible for playwork etc. Often these people are responsible for governance of a playwork provision but the supervising playworker, nominated as 'suitable person' has day-to-day management of the playwork setting. This can be problematic when this playworker is responsible for the quality of playwork but has no control over such things as budget, recruitment, working conditions, work ethic etc. We have come across a lot of people recently asking if there is specific training for playwork managers. They say that generic management training is useful up to a point, but it doesn't touch on the issues that are peculiar to managing playwork projects and settings. Perhaps this could be said by other sectors too, but certainly playwork has some unique concerns and outcomes that cause unique managerial effects.

Managers in all fields of work have to:

1 budget, plan for and oversee financial resources
2 recruit, select and keep staff
3 manage and develop staff
4 monitor and evaluate projects and programmes
5 access and manage information and resources
6 communicate and network with other professionals/sectors
7 oversee that the work of the organization is properly carried out.

Looking at this last point, in playwork it is crucial for a manager to have a true and working understanding of playwork otherwise s/he will not understand the additional issues that each of the others raise. Let's take these issues one at a time.

Finance

There is very little statutory playwork provision in the United Kingdom, which means that managers are often heavily involved in ongoing fund-raising and having to compete for funds. Very often these funds also have other agendas such as health, crime prevention etc. which means that projects have to satisfy other criteria and provide evidence of doing so – this does not just involve extra time and monitoring, but it can also affect or dilute playwork practice if not well managed and if the aims and values of playwork are not clarified before, during and at the end of a project's life.

The other side of the coin is that sometimes money becomes unexpectedly available and has to be spent in inappropriate timescales and then more often than not suddenly ceases. This makes planning and managerial oversight very complex – playwork projects rarely enjoy long-term funding.

Recruitment

One of the difficulties here is that as an emerging sector, playwork is not well-paid and its career structure is still being established in many areas. Attracting and keeping good workers is not easy. Very often too, managers may find themselves on interviewing and short listing panels with others who are less aware of playwork's ethos, principles and value base and who want to appoint entirely different people – many of whom probably look fabulous on paper and seem to say all the right things. But how many of us know people who can 'talk the talk' but cannot 'walk the walk'? How many of us know people who have playwork qualifications but nevertheless seem to know very little about playwork?! Recruitment is not straightforward!

A further issue is that many projects also rightly feel that children themselves should have as much, if not more say, in the appointment of people who will be working directly with them and generic recruitment and selection courses don't instruct participants in how to do this to (a) ensure a fair appointment and (b) ensure genuine – not tokenistic – children's participation!

Managing and developing staff

While proper staff development procedures around induction, supervision and appraisal should be in place, playwork managers regularly find they need to adapt these to incorporate Playwork Principles and the reflective practice that needs to be done both individually and as a team. For a team of playworkers to do good playwork, it will involve open and honest communication, peer observation and a strong commitment to self-awareness and support of others – this requires a different style of management that is much more democratic.

Another ongoing issue is access to playwork training and qualifications and scope for continuous professional development. This can often be a postcode lottery, with opportunities, choice and quality varying hugely across the United Kingdom. Misunderstanding by inspectors, employers and funders alike has meant that childcare qualifications get the lion's share of funding and that in some areas playwork qualifications are not even available. In other areas, playwork training and assessment providers exist but are poorly staffed by people of dubious competence and experience. Sometimes funding is made available for such training as First Aid, Child Protection or Food Hygiene, but not for playwork-specific training. This all makes training needs analysis and staff development far more complex for a playwork manager than it might for a manager in a related sector.

Monitoring and evaluating

There is much that is useful in terms of generic methods of monitoring and evaluating policy and practice, but again playwork managers find that (a) these need adaptation or different criteria and (b) they ask 'what' and 'how' but rarely 'why' – a fundamental question in reflective playwork practice. We can come to the wrong evaluative conclusions if we do not also examine the assumptions and beliefs that underlie our practice. The necessity in playwork for such reflection also requires that workers at all levels should be involved in monitoring and evaluating and indeed in the decisions of what to monitor and why – this again calls for a different kind of management than that presented in many generic courses.

Accessing and managing information and resources

Playwork-specific information and resources are less mainstream and come from a whole range of ever-increasing sources – managers need to tap into many different networks to stay up to date and to find things out. Playwork 'resources' are also not just purchasable – they include people, ideas, skill-sharing, scrounged, borrowed and recycled equipment, materials and scrap that no other sector seems to use or consider. Managing (and storing!) such resources, requires co-operative and co-ordination skills rarely covered in generic management training.

Communicating with other professionals

The major difficulty here is that many other professional people still do not consider play-workers and managers of playworkers as professional equals. This means that playwork managers have to develop broader skills in diplomacy, assertiveness, advocacy, initiative-taking, communication and research, not to mention emotional self-management.

Having to liaise regularly and professionally with inspectors, teachers, social workers, youth workers, police officers, health workers, etc. is a highly skilled job, especially when it is not unusual for them to think that playworkers are less qualified or untrained do-gooders, misguided hippies, ignorant activists or dangerous communists (we have experienced all of these!). As playwork overall covers almost the entire age range of a child, it straddles other sectors and many playworkers are highly skilled and knowledgeable professional people dealing with a wide range of people and events. Sadly this is still often unrecognized and playwork managers do have to liaise with and respond to diverse people and situations with a wider array of specific skills that generic management courses are not promoting or covering.

Oversight of delivery

Perhaps the main issue here is that in playwork it is crucial that managers stay occupationally competent and in touch with the realities of face-to-face work. In practice, this will mean managers taking time to simply be in the play environments they oversee. This will inevitably mean relating to children and 'getting down and dirty' as well as taking opportunities to observe uses of space and materials by children and by staff; see the relationships and interventions between staff and children and the impact of these; watch the management of risk and other legal procedures in action. This periodic but regular closeness to the interface is essential if managers are to understand ongoing playwork practice and properly support their staff and volunteers.

Reflection opportunity

So what is your particular experience of playwork management? You could be a senior local government manager with responsibility for dozens of projects. You could be a middle manager overseeing anything from a couple to a score of settings. You could be a manager of one major project or playground with a variety of full-time and part-time staff. You could be a member of a management committee. ⇨

> You could manage a small setting with a couple of workers. You could be someone who observes and liaises with playwork managers. You could be a playworker who has to manage their manager.
>
> Do the Playwork Principles also underpin and guide your management – or your manager? Have you recognized and understood the additional skills and issues that are needed to effectively manage playworkers and playwork settings? Are there more you can add?

A look at the levels 3 (supervisory) and 4 (managerial) national occupational standards for playwork are quite telling because in describing the job function for a competent playworker at these levels, it reveals just how much knowledge, understanding and skill is required. This is also due to the fact that playwork provision cannot be 'cloned'. Each setting – its ambience, spaces and resources should genuinely reflect the ongoing and ever-changing individual and group play needs of children and young people in that particular cultural and geographical neighbourhood. This requires specific skills in

1 advocacy
2 networking
3 research
4 analysis
5 design
6 facilitation
7 communication
8 dynamic risk assessment
9 intervention
10 observation
11 reflection

It also requires values in equality, co-operation, inclusion with a profound respect for children and a deep commitment to their rights. The level 4 NVQ in playwork and some of the BA Playwork degree courses available cover some aspects of playwork management but in a somewhat ad hoc manner as much of the information pertaining to management-specific skills and knowledge is included in the optional units or modules. Neither the NVQ nor degrees have 'management of playwork' as their raison d'etre. Perhaps a compulsory mini playwork management award, suitable for all types of playwork managers, would not only help with the quality of playwork provided for children but might also help raise the status of playwork as a profession, thereby also improving the general pay and conditions of all playworkers. This seems to be one of those 'chicken and egg issues'. Should there be more emphasis on the 'management' of playwork thereby potentially improving the quality of practice or should there be more emphasis on the quality assurance aspects of playwork thereby better promoting the need for good management in playwork? What do you think?

Useful contacts

www.londonplay.org.uk

www.ncb.org

www.playwales.org.uk

www.skillsactive.com/playwork (national occupational standards)

www.skillsactive.com/playworkprinciples

www.surestart.gov.uk

References

Best Play (2000) *Best Play*. London: National Playing Fields Association (available from www.ncb.org.yk/dotpdf/open%20
access%20-%20phase%201%20only/bestplay_cpc_20040115.pdf)

Hughes, B. (2001) *First Claim – A Framework for Quality Playwork Assessment*. Cardiff: Play Wales.

Playwork National Occupational Standards available from www.skillsactive.com/training/standards

Quality in Play (1999) *Quality in Play*. London: NCB.

Scrutiny Group (2004) *Playwork Principles*. www.skillsactive.com/playworkprinciples.

Surestart (2003) *National Standards for Out of School Care*. Nottingham: Department for Education and Skills.

8 Playwork and Other People

Playwork does not exist in a vacuum. It operates alongside many other services that exist for children and also in a variety of places, which sometimes means there are competing and conflicting perspectives about what playworkers should be doing. Good playwork managers will understand the importance of working in conjunction with other individuals and organizations. Not only because of the requirements of statutory regulations and criteria for quality assurance schemes but also because there are real benefits to be had for both children and playwork provision as a whole, by working together with others. In this chapter we will consider some of these links and also some of the perceptions that others have of playwork and the effects that these perceptions have on the health of playwork as a profession. We shall also reflect upon what the far-reaching consequences might be for society if the playwork ethos and approach were more widely understood.

Recognition of playwork

Many playworkers report that they have been at social events and have been asked what they do for a living and inwardly groaned at the question. Many in the general public understand childcare and they understand education, but they look quizzical or glaze over when given an explanation of what a playworker is and does. (See Chapter 1.) Very often this is the kind of response that is given. 'So you play with children? Sounds like a cushy job. . . .' Hence the inner groan – partly at their lack of understanding and partly at our lack of articulation. Many playworkers choose to describe themselves as something other in order to avoid the problem. I (Jacky) often say in answer to questions about what I do 'I train adults who work with children in places where they play' or 'I write about children's play' or some such that avoids using the word playwork. When I reflect on this I feel guilty. How have I advanced understanding?

Key question

If you are a playworker reading this chapter, how do you describe yourself and the work that you do, to people outside of playwork? If you are a non-playwork person, what have your previous perceptions (if any) of playwork been?

Playwork has been very poor at promoting itself, but it has to – collectively and individually – become more succinct at explaining what playwork is and what the playwork ethos is to a society that, at times, seems not only to have forgotten the importance of play, but seems to prize more highly children's grades and good behaviour than children's self-esteem and search for meaning.

Recognition of playwork as a profession in its own right is slowly growing, thanks to the ongoing hard work of various individuals and play/playwork organizations. Some departments in the different UK Governments and Assemblies have recently begun to champion play but many in the playwork world are sceptical about whether the play to which they refer in their papers is the type of play that playworkers believe is important.

Play happens in many places (see below) and most adults, both in and out of the Children's Workforce have their own views about play and its value. (See Chapter 2.) So we have the play of children at home; the play of Early Years; the play of Youth Justice; the play of Education; the play of Health; the play of Architecture and so on and each of these will use their own ideas or theories and/or statistical information that will suit their own purposes and will give them their own vision of what play is, what it is for and how to respond or provide for it. It is therefore not hard to see why there has been such a focus in adult society on learning and development as fundamental to any playing and how this resultant paradigm has permeated thinking about what playwork 'should' be.

There is a long, long way to go, but we cherish the hope that one day playwork will be fully understood and that then there will be no need for playworkers because:

a it will be universally recognized that children need freedom and space to play and so staffed compensatory play spaces will not be required

b the ethos of playwork will be universally recognized so that any adult living or working with children will understand and know how to support and attend to playing children.

In the meantime, we should continue to provoke and nurture such understanding to the community at large and particularly to parents and carers and others within the Children's Workforce, where it is vital not only for the well-being of children and their play, but also for the continued well-being of playwork. This was recognized in the Summary of Ideas of the Futures in Playwork Project (a partnership project that provided a platform for creative discussion, from the entire UK playwork world about what the future of playwork should be) where it was stated that 'adult attitudes to play are crucial as they frequently give permission to play (or not) in the local environment' and in the section on Shifting Public Perception the suggestion that 'children's play should be seen as different to their education, with a different approach, ethos, theory and practice' (2008).

The lack of understanding has led to the 'adulteration' of play in most settings that are not playwork settings and to playworkers being at the mercy of other adult agendas. Thus management committees of community led play provision, senior managers of local authority play provision, privately managed organizations etc. have often put their own stamp on the playwork provision, turning it into something that it should not be and that certainly is not playwork.

This lack of wider recognition currently means then, that playwork exists in a number of places, but:

1 often not with equal geographical distribution
2 sometimes sadly more often by default than design, and
3 sometimes in name only (i.e. people are called playworkers but are not actually doing playwork).

The playwork sector

Playwork can be found in local authorities, voluntary organizations and the private sector.

Playworkers can be found in holiday playschemes, adventure playgrounds, play ranger projects, before and after school clubs, play centres and mobile play projects. Playwork can be found in schools, prisons, hospitals, forests, parks, nurseries, community centres, youth clubs, playgrounds, refuges, leisure centres and on buses, streets and beaches. This is understandable of course, because wherever children can or do play, there may be playworkers too. But it also means it is both harder for playwork to be recognized in its own right and it is easier for it to be tainted with or overtaken by other adult agendas like crime prevention, health and education.

Playwork has never fitted very comfortably into one Government or Local Authority Department or work sector. This is for various reasons (some previously mentioned) such as:

1 Venues – as we have seen, playwork happens in a variety of different places that belong to different private and charitable organizations, local government departments, etc.
2 Employers – playworkers are employed by diverse sectors such as social services, education, sport and recreation, parks and gardens, health, travel agencies, breweries, banks, corporate and multi-national businesses etc.

3 Funding – playwork is locally organized with any funding that comes from any funding stream whose outcomes can be deemed to fit – so, for instance many playschemes and playworker remuneration are funded by church or other faith funding, return to work schemes, crime prevention budgets etc.,

4 Raison d'etre – playwork often happens alongside or as part of other work with children. For example a family drug rehabilitation centre may employ a 'children's worker' to provide play and support for the children of drug abusers.

5 This adds to the confusion in relation to exactly what playwork is and what playworkers do both inside and outside of the playwork profession. Even the word 'profession' is the subject of debate and hotly contested discussion. Is playwork a process, an approach, a profession, a function? As you may have realized by now playwork is political! Playworkers work with children, but are they and/ or should they be part of the wider political agenda of the Children's Workforce?

There are two driving forces within the playwork sector pushing for wider recognition. The first comes from a purist stance and pushes for professional status of playwork in its own right with its own dedicated theory base and its own purpose-built play spaces, separate from the rest of the Children's Workforce. The second feels that this approach is too isolationist and exclusive and will sound the death knell of playwork, so they push for promoting the uniqueness of the playwork approach, that is, an understanding of self-directed play and how to support it, into other sectors working with children and young people.

Neither of these 'forces' are wholly right or wrong of course; there is truth and validity in both and both are committed to the survival of playwork and to children's rights to play (though both would do well to remember this!).

As you may by now expect even the supporting infrastructure of playwork is diverse and confusing and comes under various different devolved UK Government Departments. For instance, the main two in England, but not exclusively being the Department for Children, Schools and Family (DCSF) and the Department for Culture Media and Sport (DCMS). Also at the time of writing

1 SkillsActive is the Sector Skills Council responsible for playwork training and qualifications and along with other national play organizations such as Play England, Play Wales, Play Scotland and Playboard Northern Ireland, lobbies for recognition of play and playwork.

2 The Children's Play Information Service is responsible for disseminating and providing information that is relevant to playwork.

3 The Children's Play Policy Forum is responsible for policy and research related to play and playwork.

4 The National Children's Bureau funds Play England who offer regional support for playwork and also produce a free publication 'Play Today'.

5 KIDS runs The Play Inclusion Project which promotes and provides for disabled children.

6 The 4 Nations Child Policy Network now operates as 4 linked websites (see references) on behalf of Children in Scotland; Children in Northern Ireland; Children in Wales and National Children's Bureau (England.)

7 There are also a number of other national and charitable organizations such as Fair Play, (supporting Children's Rights) JNCTP (supporting playwork education and training and promoting playwork), Playlink (multifaceted play consultancy) Free Play Network (a discussion forum for playworkers) and playworkforum, a Virtual Community for playworkers.

On occasions the work of these major national organizations that influence playwork, overlaps or is in direct opposition to each other. It is therefore sometimes difficult for playworkers to see the whole picture. If it is difficult from within the playwork world we can see just how easily playwork can be misunderstood from the outside and how easily it can be manipulated.

Playwork relationships with parents and carers

What is the relationship between playworkers and parents and carers? How does each view the other? The answer to this will depend upon: our current societal attitudes to children; political influences and considerations; the setting; the values and policies of the setting; the skills of the playworkers and the wishes of the parents. Different parents will want different amounts of interaction with the playwork setting. Here are some that we have experienced and seen.

Parents and carers who:

1 see playwork as childcare – they want their children to be looked after safely and that is their priority
2 are friendly and interested in what goes on in the setting as well as the welfare of their own children – they show an interest in play
3 see the setting as a place for their children to further their education and want visible developmental outcomes
4 constantly complain about issues such as dirty clothes, perceived bullying, inappropriate activities, perceived lack of safety etc.
5 are too busy to show interest in the setting or their child's involvement with it and only deliver and/or collect their children
6 are not involved with the setting at all, never visit it or show any interest or concern – the setting is somewhere for their children to go
7 want to volunteer and work in or on behalf of the setting
8 want to hang around and chat but are not interested in what goes on.

Key question

Can you think of any other interactions that parents and carers have with playworkers?

In each of the home countries we are guided by parliamentary acts and frameworks that potentially affect our relationships with parents, such as, for example,

1 Every Child Matters, Early Years Foundation Stage Standards and The Children's Plan in England
2 Getting it right for every child: Draft Children's Services Bill in Scotland

3 All Wales Child Protection Procedures in Wales
4 Children Order Guidance and Regulations for Family Support, Childminding and Day Care Centres
   in Northern Ireland, to work in partnership with parents.

We must consider exactly what these kinds of frameworks mean for playwork. Obviously parents are important to children and both parents and children have rights. Parents and carers are seen as key partners in children's lives and as such it is important to exchange information with them about the child and his welfare. Positive relationships with parents are essential. However the nature of these relationships could have an effect on how the children engage in the setting.

In her chapter on networking, (2003:151) Martin considers a case study of a local play project which has a reputation of being 'a friendly place for parents and carers to have a "cuppa and a chat"' and this is seen as a way to forge better relationships that lead to some parents becoming volunteers. It also puts the play project at the heart of the local community. However she also states that 'some playworkers argue the play project is a place to escape from the parent's watchful eye' and the involvement of parents and carers under these circumstances is unwelcome. When parents become involved in a management committee the relationship can become further complicated.

Our current social construction of children's position in society is of them in a family where the responsibility of parents is stressed. Moss and Petrie (2002:103) however suggest that 'rather than focusing on the child in her family, we would choose to view children as part of a wider network of relationships' and 'In this way we would decentre the family, recognising that childhood is lived in a variety of settings, each with its own set of relationships'. Some playworkers believe that the child benefits more from their play experiences and their time within the play provision if the parents have no involvement. This leaves the child free to be herself, to play and make friends in her own way and to develop independence.

Parents need to be informed but should they also be involved in the play setting? Is playwork by necessity a form of community work, involving the wider community and particularly parents and carers or should it concentrate solely on children and their play?

Japanese adventure playgrounds are a part of their community. They have no fences and often have public paths crossing them. Adults are welcome to visit and playworkers see it as part of their job to enable other adults, parents or otherwise, to facilitate play while enabling children to remain in control of their environment. This makes play very public and also promotes dialogue between the generations. The adventure playground is a resource for the whole community.

Playworkers have a role to advocate for play and some would argue that it is part of that role to involve parents and carers in the work in order that they may learn about the positive effects of play and how to provide for it. Certainly we have a role to help them understand about the importance of play, its benefits, and the best way that they can provide for it in their homes and in their relationship with their children.

Photo 8.1 Playing on holiday.

Reflection – Ali

I initiated and established a local community playscheme at my son's school. The headteacher was very co-operative and supportive which was half the battle and the whole scheme – which ran for two weeks for about 120 children each summer for several years – was staffed by local parents who had never done anything like this before. We met several times throughout the year at my house and at the pub and I was fortunate to have a group who were hardworking, lots of fun and willing to have a go. They would never have called themselves playworkers but essentially that's what many of them became and whenever I bump into any of them now, they will still talk animatedly about the great fun had by all at the time, but also the long-term effects on both themselves (many of them ended up retraining and going into the Children's Workforce as a result) and their children who had experiences they would never have otherwise had.

Key question

How can we work in partnership with parents in such a way that we raise their awareness of the importance of play without increasing the likelihood of adulteration of the play experience that the children are having at the play provision?

Here are some real examples, that we have also seen work, that involve parents and carers in the play setting without adulterating the children's play experiences:

1 Invite parents to an open play session to play with their own child. The child plans what they are going to play and how they are going to play. This can also involve joining with other children and their parents to play in groups if that is what the children decide on.

2 Have a regular time and space, perhaps once a month where parents can come to the play setting and chat to the playworkers either alone or as a group and occasionally have specific speakers or topics about play and playwork.

3 Have occasional sessions where the child may invite a friend or a parent to the session (if the setting is not open access, this needs careful planning in advance to check insurance, ratios etc.).

4 Have clear written information about your ethos and approach to play so that parents can clearly understand what the setting is about. Other leaflets, booklets, magazines and books about play would also help for anyone interested.

5 Involve parents in peripheral but important activities that will benefit the provision such as fund raising, scrap collection, lobbying, printing leaflets etc.

6 If you really want to offer opportunities for volunteering the following might help –

- Publicize local courses related to playwork and encourage interested parents and carers to attend. This would then enable you to offer them placement opportunities while studying but with built-in quality control related to the work they do.
- Have a very clear, very tight policy for volunteering that clarifies the relationship of parents and carers with their child while working. Include the work they can do and the work they can't do and interview and induct all volunteers and have regular supervision sessions.

Reflection – Jacky

I have had many experiences of trying to help playwork organizations sort out problems that involve playworkers working on the project where their own children attend. This seems to cause three main problems. Either the parent playworkers are too harsh with their own child, presumably with the idea that nobody can accuse them of favouritism, or too soft with their own child either by being over-protective or by giving them their own way all the time, or they try to have nothing to do with their own child. None of these strategies work very well. For parent playworkers to be effective they must have a fair and equal approach to working with all the children including their own. Without support and mentoring this can be very difficult for some parents.

Playwork and the local community

'*It takes a village to raise a child*' (an un-attributable African proverb suggesting that child rearing is the job of the whole community and not just that of the primary carers).

Children are members of communities. 'The child's development is a process of individual and group construction' (2002:103). However much that has been termed 'playcare' and which employs most of the people who are termed playworkers (64%) (2006:18) is isolated from its communities and often happening in special places set aside and out of the eyes of local people. This may be a good thing from the point of view of children being able to play in their own way and without the interference of adults, but should it not be the children themselves who make the decision about that which should be separate and that which is played out in public. Children in Japanese adventure playgrounds seem to cope very well.

In the past and before the environment took on its current perceived dangerous state, many children frequently 'played out' in the eyes of the local community within a local neighbourhood. The people in the local community do not have the same power that other professionals and parents have over children's lives, in fact they could be seen to be a resource for play and as such should be made available, by the provision, to compensate for their possible lack of availability in some children's lives. Obviously a local community will have both positive and negative facets and children will be more or less welcome and safe in different communities.

Here are some examples of how a playwork provision can help children to better integrate into their local neighbourhood:

1 If most of the children at the setting are ferried around by car from one place to another you could use local transport or walking when going on trips out or have options to go for a local walk.

2 Use local shops with the children and get to know the shopkeepers – they will then get to know and get used to the children and probably end up donating unused newspapers, boxes etc. to your setting.

3 Use local facilities (if there are any) wherever and whenever possible such as community centres; local parks and green spaces; local swimming pools; local libraries.

4 Have options for occasional escorted treasure/scavenger hunts; taking photographs out in the community; making a newsletter and interviewing local people etc.

5 Invite local people with something to offer into the setting – use their talents.

6 Have the occasional local community session (this may involve publicizing to a whole community or inviting one particular group at a time, for example, senior citizens, local dog owners, community police etc.) where the children can plan what they think is appropriate such as tea and buns; a performance of some kind; involving people in games, quizzes, activity etc.

7 Have an open evening or day when the children are not there and have displays and information about what you do, the importance of play and how people from the local community could help. Most people enjoy reminiscing about their own play and this can be a way of engaging them. Have some different types of resources from across the eras for people to look at and think about.

Reflection – Ali

I came across a couple of examples recently that illustrate how reclaiming use of local facilities by children has positive effects. Supervised regular trips to the local swimming baths means that children get known by the pool staff and so are more likely to be tolerated and even welcomed when they then go on their own. A playworker told me how if children genuinely misbehave when they go on their own, the pool manager now contacts her about it rather than the parents so that she can follow it up. Similarly she told me that when recent new pool staff were throwing their weight about and rather aggressively and unnecessarily telling children off, the said children felt secure enough to make their own complaint to the pool manager who then had a word with the staff.

The same setting also has regular escorted trips to a local park, which has a large dell with bushes and trees where the children love to play but their parents don't allow them to go there on their own. However because they go regularly with the play setting, the children feel over time that they have now gained some 'ownership' of the park. I was there recently walking to the park with a group from the setting and was both amused and pleased when just after arrival in the park, two of the older children rushed off to the dell and then came flying back announcing to the playworker that they 'had done the pervy check and the coast was clear'!

Playwork and other professionals

Playworkers increasingly have to work as part of multidisciplinary teams, even those who would like to remain separate from others within the Children's Workforce will eventually have to work to the Children Act (2004) which gives responsibilities to all children's services providers to work together in an integrated way and to focus on early identification of children's support needs. This involves such things as are already in practice in England:

1 information sharing systems
2 a common assessment framework
3 a tiered model of need that includes all children's services
4 The Extended Schools agenda has meant that many out of school clubs that used to operate independently now have a close relationship with their feeder schools and this can involve both school staff and governors.

Many local authorities have Play Strategies and it is good practice for these to be developed and implemented with involvement from all key stakeholders. This includes all children's services and the faith sector, community organizations and other interested parties.

All of the above requires playworkers to work with other professionals and it is therefore important if we wish to be taken seriously:

1 to act as advocates for children's play
2 to have influence and to halt the tide of adulteration
3 present ourselves, and playwork in a united, professional, informed and informative, way.

It is also important that we, within playwork, are able to identify that which is within the remit of playwork and that which belongs to others. We may have views about many things connected to children but that does not make us experts in all those. We would do well to remember that if we state our opinions as truths without substantiation we may not be taken seriously by other professionals. We owe children the right to have knowledgeable, well-informed and skilled playworkers advocating for their play.

Playwork is at a pivotal point in its existence. If the English Government's Children's Plan and Play Strategy that emanates from it are successful and if various initiatives, such as the Futures in Playwork Project which are currently being undertaken that relate to playwork lead to improvements, then employment opportunities in playwork should soar. We wait with bated breath.

So if playwork were fully understood and, as suggested above, there was no need for playworkers, perhaps our society would be one where there would be an emphasis on 'personal fulfilment, communal values and quality of life' (1997:234). Perhaps play for both children and adults, would be seen to be as essential as education and more essential than work. Play makes us happy and it can happen anywhere, at any time and it is free. Work on the other hand can cause us stress and it often goes over time and eats into our pleasure time. In our playwork vision of society work would be kept in its place and children and adults creativity, physicality and spirituality would be celebrated through play.

Many of the public spaces in the community would be play places for children, young people and adults and each would respect the need for communal and separate times for playing. There would be no 'no-go' areas such as there currently are and traffic would be either kept away or 'calmed' from the community play places.

Is this an unrealistic vision or is it one that society is currently demonstrating that it needs. Is the current drive towards more extreme sports for adults a sign of play deprivation? Is petty crime such as graffiti, joy riding, happy slapping and increase in bullying a sign of play deprivation? Is the rise in alcoholism in young people, focus on celebrity and the media a sign of play deprivation?

Key question

What do you think? Can a playwork approach to play help children to be well rounded and grounded adults?

Photo 8.2 The joy of playing.

'Play isn't just for children . . . Play is for all of us, helping us to go on making good the past and preparing for the future, helping to restore the balance between inner and outer tensions and pressures and once the balance has been restored, making it possible for us to grow and develop in harmony with ourselves and others.'

Crowe (1983:21)

Useful contacts

Children in Scotland www.childpolicyinfo.childreninscotland.org.uk

Children in Northern Ireland www.cpinfo.ofg.uk

Children in Northern Ireland www.ci-ni.org.uk

Children in Wales www.childreninwales.org.uk

SkillsActive www.skillsactive.com

National Children's Bureau www.ncb.org.uk

Children's Play Information Service www.ncb.org.uk/cpis

Children's Play Council now Play England Council www.ncb.org.uk/cpc

Kids www.kids.org.uk

Fair Play for children www.arunet.co.uk/fairplay/

Playlink www.playlink.org.uk

Free Play Network www.freeplaynetwork.org.uk

UK Playworkers http://groups.yahoo.com/group/UKplayworkers

References

Crowe, B. (1983) *Play is a Feeling*. London: George Allen and Unwin.

Davy, A. and Gallagher, J. (2006) *New Playwork Play and Care for Children 4–16*. London: Thomson.

Martin, J. (2003) 'It's Not What You Know, but Who You Know' in Brown, F. (Eds) *Playwork Theory and Practice*. Buckingham: Open University Press.

Moss, P. and Petrie, P. (2002) *From Children's Services to Children's Spaces*. London: Routledge Farmer.

Abrams, R. (1997) *The Playful Self: Why Women Need Play in Their Lives*. London: 4th Estate.

SkillsActive (2006) *Playwork People 2: Research into the Characteristics of the Playwork Workforce*. London: SkillsActive.

9 Playwork Education and Training

In this final chapter we will look at what is involved in building an educated, trained and qualified workforce and what is currently happening in the playwork sector in relation to this.

Playwork has come a long way in forty years. It has made many passionate claims that have come from intuitive practice and personal experience without always having the evidence for these. Much as many in the sector might like to claim that play is the panacea for all ills – that is, if children truly have the freedom to play then they would be:

1 physically fitter,
2 emotionally more resilient and capable,
3 thinking more critically and creatively,
4 socially more competent,
5 more empathic,
6 psychologically healthier,
7 more independent and assertive,
8 better behaved, and
9 generally wiser.

It is still not a proven fact even though seasoned playworkers feel it is obviously true! But there is now a growing academic playwork discipline that is properly researching these claims in wider literature reviews and a scrutiny of practice and while we cannot absolutely confirm that play guarantees future survival and development, we can be quite certain that it definitely helps! Lester and Russell's recent publication is useful and heady reading on this score (2008).

There has been growing concern over the last few years however, about children in general; their behaviour, their health, their literacy. These concerns – and others – were highlighted in Sue Palmer's book *Toxic Childhood*. UK Governments have been slowly recognizing that life for children has considerably changed in the last few decades and not necessarily for the better. As a result of evolving policies to improve the situation, playwork has just begun to benefit from increased funding and support from a variety of sources and there is presently real hope for change.

Employment in playwork

SkillsActive has done the most comprehensive research into employment in playwork (2006). Their findings suggest that the playwork workforce is predominantly female (88%) but that this is gradually changing and playworkers with ethnic minority backgrounds and with impairments are underrepresented. The workforce is predominantly part-time with 21.6 being the average number of hours worked in the sector per week and that not surprisingly a high proportion of playworkers have more than one job in the sector or an additional job(s) in other sectors.

As we saw in Chapter 1, playworkers work in a wide range of settings and many playwork jobs are considered hard to fill because of a shortage of suitably qualified and experienced playwork people and lack of specific skills. We list later which playwork qualifications are currently acceptable and nationally recognized. Some of the skills that employers considered important in all areas of playwork are:

1 team working
2 communication
3 maintaining safety
4 initiative
5 customer service (one assumes that this means children and not just their parents)
6 ability to follow instructions
7 personal appearance and attitude
8 planning and preparing work
9 problem solving
10 knowledge of Playwork Principles (this was not high on the list)

Having read this far and understood the external misperceptions of playwork, you will not be surprised by now to see that the employers have not included some of those aspects of skills that we in the sector consider vital, such as:

1 ability to reflect on their work and make changes to their working practices based on this
2 knowledge about play
3 knowledge about how to create and provide play environments
4 adaptability and flexibility

Currently the pay and terms and conditions of employment for playworkers are governed in an ad hoc way and are dependent upon the employing organization and sources of funding or revenue. In 2005 research carried out by SkillsActive (2006:16–17) suggested that the median pay for playworkers was £5.75p per hour – this ranged from £1.50 an hour for a playworker (in a profit-making enterprise) and £18 an hour for the manager of a play setting. The current minimum wage is £5.73 an hour for over 22-year-olds and £4.77 for over 18-year-olds and therefore these would be the minimum hourly rates a playworker could expect. Obviously some get paid more and certainly play supervisors or co-ordinators can expect to earn rates of over £7.50 an hour. But it is certainly unregulated and somewhat of a lottery. At the time of writing for example, Ali knows of two local projects – one is a private business paying a basic rate of £5.70 an hour for contact time only and the other is a voluntary organization promoting inclusive play in schools and pays its basic workers £9.60 an hour which includes as many hours spent planning and evaluating as working face to face.

SkillsActive research suggests that the average working hours for a playworker in a playwork setting is 21½ hours per week. Employment patterns obviously differ for playworkers working at before and after-school clubs, holiday playschemes, adventure playgrounds or specialist play facilities. Some playworkers are only paid for their face to face work with children while others are also paid for planning, organization, reflection and meetings. One thing is for sure, the professional, vocational and educational standards imposed on playworkers have increased manifold, however the pay and conditions have not kept pace with these requirements.

Training and qualifications

In the process of building the evidence and theoretical base for playwork, training and qualifications in playwork have proliferated but also become more rationalized.

SkillsActive is the Sector Skills Council responsible for playwork. All awarding bodies offering playwork qualifications and all organizations or training providers wanting recognition of training courses they have developed have had to go through SkillsActive for peer endorsement. This has been hugely important in trying to ensure as far as possible that the content of training and qualifications is underpinned by Playwork Principles and values, espouses current playwork theory and is mapped against the national occupational standards for playwork.

SkillsActive has also:

a set up various quality assurance initiatives and requirements to equally try and ensure that trainers, assessors and verifiers around the United Kingdom are occupationally competent and up to date

b set up various UK-wide committees to work towards and oversee national developments such as:

1 occupational standards at levels 2, 3 and 4
2 co-operation and co-ordination between awarding bodies offering playwork qualifications
3 playwork in higher education
4 endorsement and approval of new training and qualifications in playwork

c explored various ways to support and recognize continuing professional development in playworkers

d developed transitional awards in order to 'fast-track' either early years workers or playworkers into each other's sectors and are currently also looking at similar awards for youth workers.

Qualifications presently available are:-

CACHE (Council for Awards in Childcare and Education)

Level 2 Award, Certificate and Diploma in Playwork
Level 2 NVQ in Playwork
Level 3 Award, Certificate and Diploma in Playwork
Level 3 NVQ in Playwork
Level 3 Award in Playwork for Early Years and Child Care Workers

City and Guilds

Level 2 Certificate and Diploma in Playwork
Level 2 NVQ in Playwork
Level 3 Certificate and Diploma in Playwork
Level 3 NVQ in Playwork
Level 3 Award in Playwork for Early Years and Child Care Workers
Level 4 NVQ in Playwork

Edexcel

Levels 2 & 3 NVQ in Playwork

SQA (Scottish Qualifications Authority)

Level 2 SVQ in Playwork
Level 3 SVQ in Playwork
National Progression Awards in Playwork
Level 2 Award, Certificate and Diploma in 'Playwork Principles into Practice'

There are also a number of higher education universities offering diplomas, foundation degrees, degrees, post-graduate certificates and diplomas, master degrees and even doctorates in playwork. Some of these are available by distance learning and e-learning. Institutions currently include (others are in development):

1   University of East London
2   City of Bristol College
3   Sheffield Hallam University
4   Northumbria University
5   Leeds Metropolitan University
6   Gloucestershire University
7   Glyndwr University (North Wales)

The national framework for all qualifications in England, Wales & Northern Ireland (Scotland has its own framework) is currently changing and there are in fact two frameworks operating at the moment – the National Qualifications Framework (NQF) and the Qualifications Credit Framework (QCF). The latter is replacing the former by 2010 and changing the nature of qualifications so that credit can be awarded to learners unit by unit as they progress through more flexible qualification routes.

This will necessarily affect almost all the awarding body qualifications listed above as most of these are on the NQF. At the time of writing, SkillsActive is proposing to work with awarding bodies to create 'common units' at different levels – this will rationalize and make the number of qualifications more manageable as all awarding bodies will agree to use the same learning outcomes but will choose different assessment methods.

We have been involved in training playworkers at all levels for many years and also in training other playwork trainers and assessors. Much is required in terms of design, content and support to enable people to successfully complete their qualifications. Sadly – as we have often seen in our experiences of external verification – other matters get in the way of offering great training and the quality of a course is often clouded or minimized by, lack of trainer knowledge related to playwork (often somewhat childcare focused), insufficient funding, time, poor learning environments and/or unsupported or inexperienced trainers.

However, we want to draw attention here to two things; learners' needs and learning styles. These should not be compromised and yet quite often they are not even properly considered.

Learners' needs

All awarding bodies state that training and assessment providers must take account of learners' needs and not disadvantage them in any way. Providers must therefore have policies and procedures that show how learners across the age range, of either gender, from any racial or cultural background, with any one of a range of disabilities; have the same opportunity to access and support to complete their course or qualification. In reality, this is far harder than we all often make out. It involves consideration of all the following:

1 building a proper infrastructure of passionate and able trainers and assessors who themselves are representative and bring their own reflections, skills and experiences to the job
2 targeting and promotion born from a genuine understanding and knowledge of local communities and local organizations
3 pre-course interviewing and selection so that no-one is set up to fail and needs are properly identified
4 extra tutorial time and ongoing support for literacy and key skills
5 using signers, interpreters, readers and writers and specific equipment like Dictaphones, hearing loops, adapted word processors etc.
6 bursaries, grants and provision of books, equipment and materials for loan
7 having practical and simple complaints and appeals procedures so that issues can be resolved earlier rather than later
8 providing resources and handouts that are ethical and culturally representative and bilingual where appropriate.

It does also involve knowing where learners are starting from. For many people coming for playwork training, we also need to consider the following as well.

Time to 'unlearn'

As we have seen throughout this book, we all come to playwork and to playing children with assumptions about the role we should take, what we are seeing and how we should respond. Very often participants take it as read that their role should be one of protecting and educating children and it takes quite a while to realize that in the context of playing, this is not just inappropriate, but damaging. Much time needs to be spent in presenting information and research that causes what we call cognitive dissonance – that is, it doesn't fit with their current perceptions of reality and it challenges their thinking. This needs to be done in a variety of interesting and stimulating ways with awareness that this can be quite a scary ride for some learners!

Time to play

Many participants – especially those who are younger – will have either lost touch with the art of freely playing and/or will have experienced play deprivation in a variety of forms. This means that time needs to be taken for people to rediscover and experience play for themselves – playworkers need to be sensitive to children and not still playing out their own agendas, but they still need to be playful people and to respond wholeheartedly to children's play cues. Training courses need to therefore incorporate games and fun and laughter – all of which reinforces their learning about play. Training also needs to include opportunities and play experiences that participants may have never had. How can playworkers be comfortable with children playing with the elements of fire and water for example, unless they have also done so and are aware of both the risks and the benefits of such playing?

While children do not play to learn, they certainly do learn from playing. The same is true of trainees in playwork and training courses themselves should be crammed with learning experiences that are playful, challenging, exhilarating, reflective and lots of fun.

Learning styles

There is not one way to learn – every participant on a training course or qualification learns in different and differing ways. All too often this is not sufficiently taken into account by trainers and assessors and participants themselves are sometimes unaware of their own personal learning styles and blame themselves for their lack of achievement. Our education system – at all levels – is very much set up to only cater for certain learning styles and so children, young people and adults who do not 'fit' are left bored and unstimulated and unable to succeed.

What are these learning styles? There are many different approaches to defining and categorizing these and they all contribute to our wider understanding of how people learn. Some come from a sensory perspective, some consider mental ordering processes, some are derived from personality types, some theorize about different kinds of intelligence. We can only briefly touch on some here but we also give references for further information.

Sensory preferences – Visual, auditory, kinesthetic

The simplest model has come via the inventors of neuro-linguistic programming (NLP) developed in America in the seventies (Bandler and Grinder, 1979). It is based on the idea – and backed up with considerable research – that we have a preferred sensory way of receiving new information, namely visual (we like to look), auditory (we like to listen) and kinesthetic (we like to actively learn by doing). If for instance, we were trying to convey the benefits of risk taking in play, some learners might learn best by watching a relevant DVD, seeing a PowerPoint presentation of facts and figures or a demonstration of risk assessment, others would prefer to hear a spoken presentation or personal anecdotes or listen to a group discussing scenarios, and still others would learn best by having a go at skateboarding or collecting and connecting up cards of facts and figures or role-playing scenarios.

Kinesthetic learners are usually the most disadvantaged as their learning style is considered least and is quite often completely foreign to the teacher who happily learnt by chalk and talk methods. Playwork training really needs to encompass all three styles as often as possible.

Perceiving and ordering – Gregorc's mind styles (2001)

Gregorc's well-researched analysis looks at how people make sense of and store new information and ideas and he proposes that we are all individually positioned along two spectrums – one for perceiving and one for ordering information. The first of these – based on how we respond to new information – moves from 'concrete' at one end (those people who are down to earth, objective and take in information physically by touch or sight etc.) to 'abstract' at the other (those who love ideas and theories, are subjective and look for connections and patterns). The second of these continuums – based on how we then organize and remember this new information – has at one end 'sequential' (those who are systematic and like a logical and ordered thought process and filing system) and at the other 'random' (those with intuitive minds like a spider in a web, flitting from one point to another in what seems to make no sense to anyone but themselves).

We are all positioned somewhere along each of these two continuums so that we each have a little of all four styles but in varying percentages and it helps both learners and teachers to know where and how much, so that both can accelerate learning through personal understanding and using diverse methods that suit different people. There are a number of simple questionnaires that learners can complete early on in a course that help them and their trainers recognize their particular styles. It is also really helpful in a group of learners – participants recognize their differences and learn to understand, adapt to and work together with each other in more vibrant and effective ways.

Multiple intelligences – Howard Gardner (1993)

Gardner defines intelligences as neural potential that can help us solve problems and be creative; this potential may or may not be activated depending on the human and physical environments we find ourselves in. In so doing, he breaks the mould of academia that only values intelligence expressed through the three R's and asks the question 'how are you smart?' rather than 'how smart are you?' He claims there are eight intelligences, all of which are equally needed in society, and that we all have differing amounts of each. They are:

Linguistic
Logical and mathematical
Spatial
Musical
Bodily/kinesthetic
Interpersonal
Intrapersonal
Naturalistic

Space does not permit us to explore further here, but we would urge you to look further at these and other models. You will personally really benefit from knowing your own learning styles and what works for you – it is part of reflective practice! If you are a teacher/trainer, you simply must explore this and get to know the learning styles of your learners – it will revolutionize your courses and change their lives.

Playwork trainers are not just people to convey facts and theories about playwork; they are also ambassadors and advocates for children and as such they need to care deeply about their craft and see themselves as mentors, guides, inspirers, enquirers, partners and equals to their learners. Just as good playworkers understand and create magical and exciting play spaces, good playwork trainers understand the need for and to create sacred learning spaces that nourish, challenge and excite those who join them there.

Continuing professional development

This is a relatively new term that describes the need for any worker in any profession to keep up to date with developments in their field of work and remain occupationally competent. It is applicable to us all, whether we are new or experienced playworkers, play development workers or officers, playwork trainers, assessors or verifiers, and playwork managers and supervisors at all levels.

How do we each do this? It will of course differ according to the job we have but essentially we each have to ask ourselves the question 'how am I keeping myself up to date with playwork theory and practice' and there will be a range of possible answers. It could include any/ all of the following:

1 Face-to-face work (paid or voluntary) – this could range from a few days a year to full-time work, in a variety of possible settings
2 Observations and recordings of play – for example, who is playing with who and with what, what cues, returns and frames are in evidence, what feelings are expressed, what risks are taken
3 Audits of play environments and play spaces – for example, what play types are accessible, what elements are available, what materials are in evidence, what loose parts are possible, which spaces are favoured and how are they used?
4 Reading books and articles – there is a growing wealth of playwork-specific reading material and much else that is relevant, depending on our role
5 Attendance at and contribution to meetings – these could be team, regional, committee, multidisciplinary, national
6 Attendance at seminars or workshops
7 In-house training
8 Reflective journal or log – recording thoughts and questions that come up in practice or in discussion or from reading
9 Attendance at conferences. For example Spirit of Adventure Play, PlayEducation, Wild & Away, Beauty of Play, Meynell Games
10 Membership of and contribution to web-based discussion groups e.g. playworkerforum@yahoogroups.co.uk
11 Subscriptions to and reading of relevant journals, for example, Play Today, Children & YP now, Ip-Dip, Playwords, Play Right

12 Perusal of and downloading of material from relevant websites
13 Membership of play organizations, for example, Fair Play, Play Wales, SkillsActive, management committee of local play project
14 Supervision carried out by people knowledgeable in playwork.

We are also required to regularly give evidence of our CPD to employers, inspectors and verifiers at appraisals, inspections and visits, which also means that we need to keep fairly comprehensive records of what we do. Increasingly there are on-line ways of doing this, for example, the Institute for Learning has such a system for its members (which include playwork trainers, teachers and lecturers who have joined) and SkillsActive has introduced Active Passports for individual playworkers which has a system to record and verify courses and qualifications undertaken. These processes however do not record the detail in the list described above and playworkers would do well to note these other aspects. A simple annual list under headings such as the bullet points above is an easy way to do this – many workers use this method.

Reflective practice

Of course reflective practice is a major part of continuing professional development. We have discussed in this book about what constitutes reflective practice and given examples throughout of our own thinking. But so far we have not said much about the different ways it can be done. Not surprisingly, people reflect in diverse ways – according to their learning styles.

Key question

Which of these words do you find yourself attracted to?

1 Drawing
2 Writing
3 Talking
4 Expressing

The chances are the one(s) you are drawn to will indicate the reflection methodology of your choice. Most people think – once they recognize that reflective practice is broader and deeper than evaluation – that it is done purely by thinking and that if it has to be recorded or evidenced that it has to be written down in some kind of diary form. This is often because on training courses, participants have been required to keep some kind of reflective log. This is fine for some people and really suits them – we have seen journals from some learners that are huge and wonderful philosophical tomes. For others however, if they are given no other way of expressing themselves, such logs will contain struggling and blunt one-liners. So what are some other methods?

Writing

People who choose to record their thinking using the written word do this because it is an extension of their thinking – they think on paper. Writing down their thinking actually gets it out of their heads and helps them progress their thinking and start to resolve the issues they are thinking about. This can be done in a number of formats and it could be private or shared:

1 Jotting down questions as they occur in a notebook and returning to them later, for example, how can I broach a particular subject with a colleague? Why did I react the way I did? What might that child's play narrative be meaning?
2 Keeping a diary – for example, of observations, actions and consequences, incidents
3 Keeping an informal journal – for example, of feelings, thoughts, questions
4 Using question and answer formats – both simple and complex
5 Making up explorative prose
6 Using third-person perspective – for example, writing from someone else's viewpoint (known or unknown) – this can help you be more objective and resolve reactions or differences
7 Using unsent letters, for example, writing to someone you are angry with in order to explore why you feel that way
8 On-line discussion forums.

Talking

For many people, to reflect is to think out loud. This may mean talking to oneself – in the car, in the bath, while walking, while working. As for the writers above – it gets their thinking out of their heads and helps shape and resolve it. Reflecting by talking is also often done with one or more other people. These could include:

1 mentors
2 managers
3 tutors
4 non-line managerial supervisors
5 critical friends
6 colleagues
7 partners
8 trusted friends
9 fellow learners

Such reflection could be formal or informal, be planned, be spontaneous, be self-initiated or prompted by someone else and could be one-to-one or in groups. It obviously happens face-to-face or on the phone, but could also be via using a Dictaphone, making a video diary or chatting on-line.

Drawing

Some people think visually and find that their ways of reflecting are either pictorial or diagrammatical by nature or prompted by illustrations, pictures or images they see. To further their thinking, they use:

1 mindmaps
2 lifelines
3 diagrams
4 pictures
5 charts
6 spidergrams
7 flowcharts
8 story boards

Expressing

Some people think actively by actually doing – being hands on and using their bodies in some way. This might include:

1 role-play – re-creating or walking through a scene or an action and taking either their own or some other person's role
2 trying out, replaying and/or freeze framing incidents to consider different outcomes or perspectives
3 mirroring – copying someone else to understand a different viewpoint or action
4 creating a game or exercise from a problem that needs resolving
5 miming scenes or actions – using no words often unearths underlying emotions and motives
6 using activities like hotseating or goldfish bowl to explore a theme or issue
7 using evaluative/reflective exercises that involve movement and activity, for example, standing on a continuum, using stickers, fingers or feet to indicate opinions, etc.

Different methods suit different people and it helps to find out 'what works best for me' which may well encompass more than one of the above styles. Different methods are also appropriate to doing alone and/or with others at various times.

Reflection opportunity

So how do you keep yourself competent and up to date? Has reading this chapter sparked ideas for you or nudged you into realizing what you can or need to do? How do you/would you carry out reflective practice?

Photo 9.1 Where can play take us?

Useful contacts

www.arunet.co.uk/fairplay – Fair Play for Children. A national play organization with lots of useful information, discussions and updates about children's play today and their rights to it.

www.businessballs.com – basic introduction to VAK and Gardner's multiple intelligences with on-line tests

www.cache.org.uk – Council for Awards in Children's Care and Education

www.childline.org.uk – a charitable organization offering information and helplines to children and young people needing help or advice

www.childrenslegalcentre.org.uk – an independent national charity concerned with law and policy affecting children and young people

www.cityandguilds.com – City & Guilds

www.cityofbristol.ac.uk – City of Bristol College

www.commonthreads.co.uk – training organization with a number of useful publications and resources

www.crin.org.uk – the Child Rights information network – committed to all aspects of children's rights, legal and otherwise

www.edexcel.com – Edexcel

www.freeplaynetwork.org.uk – a network of individuals and organizations committed to promoting free play principles and practice and access to play opportunities

www.glos.ac.uk – University of Gloucester

www.glyndwr.ac.uk – Glyndwr University, North Wales

www.gregorc.com – the site of Gregorc Associates

www.kidscape.org.uk – a charitable organization that develops training and resources for both children and adults around keeping safe from child abuse and bullying

www.kids-online.org.uk – campaigning organization offering training and up-to-date information/publications regarding the rights of disabled children and inclusive play services

www.lmu.ac.uk – Leeds Metropolitan University

www.londonplay.org.uk – great site with lots of info and practical downloadable articles/forms

www.ludemos.co.uk/members1.htm – home of therapeutic playwork – link for papers

www.ncb.org.uk/cpc – the Children's Play Council. A leading national play organization working hard to promote play and influence government policy. The site is full of useful information and lists all their publications and up and coming playwork conferences and events.

www.northumbria.ac.uk – Northumbria University

www.playeducation.com – organization created by Bob Hughes to offer training, conferences and resources in play and playwork. Site includes lists of available transcripts from PlayEd Human Development meetings over the years and publications Bob has written.

www.playengland.org.uk

www.playlink.org.uk – supports local play service providers across the country, promoting and disseminating the values and playwork practice learnt in the free play environment of adventure playgrounds. Has a list of great publications.

www.playscotland.org/

www.playwales.org.uk

useful informative websites from these national organizations

www.playwork.org.uk – the National Playwork Unit at Skillsactive supports playwork education and training and playworkers in a range of ways. It provides links to interesting websites on the links page.

www.shu.ac.uk – Sheffield Hallam University

www.sqa.org.uk – Scottish Qualifications Authority

www.uel.ac.uk – University of East London

www.unicef.org/crcartoons – a link from the main UNICEF site that has downloadable cartoons about children's rights

http://groups.yahoo.com/group/ukplayworkers – the virtual community for playworkers. A free email site for playworkers to ask questions, engage in debate, let off steam, inspire others, advertise playwork jobs, keep up to date with current playwork thinking and related politics. . . .

References

Bandler, R. and Grinder, J. (1979) *Frogs into Princes*. Moab, UT: Real People Press.

Gardner, H. (1993) *Multiple Intelligences, the Theory in Practice*. New York: Basic Books.

Gregorc, F. (2001) *The Mind Styles Model; Theory; Principles and Practice*. Columbia, Connecticut: Gregorc Associates.

Lester, S. and Russell, W. (2008) *Play for a Change*. London: Play England.

Palmer, S. (2006) *Toxic Childhood*. London: Orion.

SkillsActive (2006) *Playwork People 2 Research into the Characteristics of the Playwork Workforce*. London: SkillsActive.

Afterword

So we two have come to the end of our reflective and questioning journey through some aspects of play and playwork that we consider important. We hope that we have done justice to a subject matter that we hold dear and that you the reader have been left with a desire to delve deeper into, what for us is, the magical world of play and for playworkers is, a way of working that aims to leave children's play worlds uncontaminated by the increasingly encroaching world of regulation and constraint.

Life moves on very fast and we are keenly aware that as we finished writing some of what we have had to say is already out of date. The process of publishing has to start somewhere and 1 March 2009 is our time to hand over what we hope is a 'good read' to the people who will make publication happen.

We hear on a regular basis problems related to playwork, to do with funding; closure of play provision; changes to regulations; changes to qualifications; changes to organizational structures; changes to governing bodies; changes to quality requirements; imposed relationships between organizations that do not necessarily sit happily together and so forth, but through all of this children continue to play in spite of the angst of the adult world or sometimes because of it. There is a fear that this play may be so contaminated that it will not do the job for a child that nature intended it to do. Consider a child who continues to breathe in the air no matter how polluted it is. Her lungs may become damaged and illness may follow with the child's quality of life becoming impoverished. In much the same way, a child will continue to play no matter what her circumstances, but if there is too much regulation or if the environment is inappropriate the child's play may become damaged and the quality of her life impoverished.

For lucky children there may be no need for playwork or the playwork approach but for many more children playworkers may be the only adults who support their right to play in their own way, for their own purposes, with their own chosen props and for no known outcome other than their own internal drive. If we do not enable this to happen how will our children develop a sense of self that has not been imposed on them? How will they learn to regulate their own behaviour? Find their place among their peers? Learn how good, good fun can make them feel?

We leave you now as an adult with some questions and thoughts to reflect on, for surely play is not restricted to children alone. Adults who are playful may be better able to support children's play.

1 When did you last reclaim your own right to play? If more than twenty-four hours ago it may be time to play again!
2 When did you last support somebody else to play freely? If you can't remember, think about how to behave in order to enable this to happen.
3 When did you last actively prevent somebody else from playing? If you think you have never done this, you may be kidding yourself. If you can remember doing so consider your reasons for preventing play. Were they valid ones? Could you have handled the situation better?
4 Do you believe there are times when children should play freely; times when their play should be organized by adults; times when they should not play at all? Are your reasons for these answers valid and if so what validates them?
5 Do you think that as children grow up they should play less and less or more and more?
6 Is playing more or less important than working? What is the reasoning behind your answer?
7 Do you believe that the world would be a better or worse place if we all played more?

Index